RANTS IN tHe DARK

RANTS
IN the
DARK

*from one tired
mama to another*

Emily Writes

RANDOM HOUSE
NEW ZEALAND

RANDOM HOUSE

UK | USA | Canada | Ireland | Australia
India | New Zealand | South Africa | China

Random House is an imprint of the Penguin Random House group of
companies, whose addresses can be found at global.penguinrandomhouse.com.

Penguin
Random House
New Zealand

First published by Penguin Random House New Zealand, 2017

1 3 5 7 9 10 8 6 4 2

Cover and design by Kate Barraclough © Penguin Random House New Zealand
Illustrations by Sarah Healey © Penguin Random House New Zealand
Prepress by Image Centre Group
Printed and bound in Australia by Griffin Press, an Accredited ISO AS/NZS
14001 Environmental Management Systems Printer

A catalogue record for this book is available from the National Library
of New Zealand.

ISBN 978-0-14-377018-3
eISBN 978-0-14-377019-0

penguin.co.nz

To my precious children — I love you more than all the pages of this book. I love you more than 24. Big and little and all the bits in between. More than ice cream. This book is for you.

To my beloved husband — thank you for everything, for being everything to me. I've loved you for so long, and I'll love you even longer. This book is for you.

To every person who has shared my words and been kind to me and laughed and cried with me. You made this book happen — thank you. This book is for you.

CONTENTS

INTRODUCTION

You finally got the baby down at 11 p.m. Only for them to wake 45 minutes later. Patting and shushing and patting and shushing and patting and shushing and they're asleep again after who knows how long. You stare at them in their cot — a silent prayer — SLEEP! DAMMIT! SLEEP!

Is it 10 minutes later? An hour? They're screaming again. What was that stupid advice you heard — feed, burp, dry, bath? Why does bath come after dry? There were five things. Or was it three? Your mental checklist stops after number two. You're so sleep-deprived you literally can't count anymore.

Must be the nappy.

Fumbling, swearing, sweating, you're changing that damn nappy in the dark. White noise blaring. You're screaming silently. Baby is not screaming silently. Baby is cracking open the earth with torturous yowling and you wonder what on earth could be upsetting them so much that they need to wake the entire world.

You force a boob or bottle into their gob and: silence.

Blessed silence. Peace at last.

Now begins the feed you're quite sure they didn't need — and be prepared, it's going to take an hour and a half. Your mother said you shouldn't feed them during the night past six weeks old. The mouthy one at coffee group insists her baby has been sleeping through for months now. Grandma says formula is the only way they'll sleep all night. The news says breastfeeding is the only thing keeping them healthy. The Facebook mums say you're starting bad habits. The Facebook mums say keep doing what you're doing. The Twitter mums say thank the goddess for wine. The neighbour who you didn't even know was alive has sprung from the dead at the sound of your child screaming just to let you know that in their day, babies slept through all night and they weren't coddled! The comments on that article 'Everything Wrong With This Generation's Parents' run on a loop in your head.

You want to sleep through the damn night! But you're too damn tired to finish even one page of that book by that sleep scientist, or that other book that debunks that book by a sleep consultant, and there's a sleep trainer on TV telling you about their book, too.

You're overwhelmed and over it.

The baby is cluster feeding. What do you do?

You read my book.

Why? Because you won't find judgement here. I'm writing it at 4 a.m. for you to read at 4 a.m. My kids don't sleep either. This book is an advice-free zone. Just me and you raging at the world at 4 a.m.

Take a breath. It's going to be OK. Even if it doesn't feel like it will be. *Especially* if it doesn't feel like it will be.

If you've ever stared at your baby and silently said 'I can't do this' but then kept on doing this — this book is for you.

If you've ever murdered someone in your head for giving you unsolicited sleep advice — this book is for you.

If you've ever felt like you just *need* to cuddle your sleeping baby and then immediately thought, What the hell, am I insane? He only just got to sleep! — this book is for you.

If you've ever daydreamed about leaving the house with just your wallet and keys (instead of a 28-kilo nappy bag) — this book is for you.

If you've ever answered 'just because it just is because it is' to your toddler's 872nd question — this book is for you.

If you've ever had your breath stolen by how beautiful your precious child is — this book is for you.

If you've ever sobbed in the dark over how overwhelmed you feel — yes, this book is for you.

If you've ever wished your baby would race through this horrible stage while also crying at the thought of them ever growing up — this book, it's for you.

If you've ever cried in the shower and then dried yourself off, stood tall and faced the day like a total badass even though you were absolutely sure you had nothing left — I wrote this book for you and I salute you.

Parenting is hard. And awesome. And the best thing ever. And it's so hard. And amazing. And it's a mess of contradictions and we can't get through it alone.

Let's get through it together.

THE ONE THAT STARTED IT ALL

So about my first post — the one that started it all — here's how it happened:

In the wee small hours, soon after I'd gotten my almost-four-week-old to bed, I wrote a rant. In the dark, hunched over my crusty laptop I literally cursed at the world.

I was exhausted, hormonal and hungry. My breasts hurt and I was over it. My oldest child had quickly claimed my side of the bed in the few minutes I'd left it to resettle my bub.

I was overwhelmed. So I did what I usually do when I'm overwhelmed — I wrote about it. And the next day, in a fit of madness while the baby slept, I put it online. I chucked it on an old website I had, thinking some of my friends who had just had second babies would get a laugh out of it.

Throughout the day I went through my usual routine of trying desperately to get the four-week-old to breastfeed or nap. I couldn't find where my eldest son had hidden my phone, but I could hear it beeping throughout the day.

Eventually I found it later that night — and it was full of texts from friends and alerts from Twitter and Facebook. I was so confused — how had they seen the post? I only shared it on Twitter . . . I logged in to Wordpress and saw the stats and almost passed out. Nearly a million hits in a day!

I had written it anonymously, so only a few friends knew it was by me. Others had sent it to me saying 'This woman is nuts, you'd like her' — which I decided to take as a compliment.

The friends who did know I'd written it told me to keep writing. So I did. And here I am, writing a book, just over one year later.

Writing about parenting has kept me (somewhat) sane, it has connected me with mothers around the world, and it has made me a better parent. It has made me feel less isolated and it has made me realise that nobody is alone on their journey.

Even when it feels like it — we are not alone.

We are not alone when we are too tired to stand.

We are not alone when we despair over what seems like a complete inability to feed our child, whether it's at the breast or at the dinner table.

We are not alone when we stare in horror as our child has a complete meltdown in the supermarket, quietly muttering 'I wonder where the mother is' to the mean old lady who is shaking her head at 'kids these days'.

We are not alone when we stare in wonder at our sleeping baby but then do a ninja roll and almost break our legs when their closed eyelids twitch.

We are not alone when we scream JUST GO TO SLEEP PLEASE in our head.

We are not alone when we drink the last cold drops of our coffee and wish we could just eat a meal alone.

You've got a village. It might not feel like it, but you do. We are all in this together, and every mother has blinked back tears at the agony and beauty of this most important job we have.

You're not alone. You're never alone.

Especially when some dickfritter tells you to be grateful, when you should be allowed to just say 'FUCK OFF! I HAVE NOT SLEPT IN TWO YEARS!'

I AM GRATEFUL, NOW FUCK OFF

It was some time between midnight and 3 a.m. I was dead asleep. I'd fed the littlest at midnight, so it was after that, and it was before he woke up for a feed at 3 a.m. This hardly matters, because that time of night is hell unless you're pashing, happy drunk, smoking in a bar or dancing on a bar — y'know, generally having a fulfilling life that doesn't involve milk dripping out of your breasts or playing the 'fart or shit?' game.

So, I'm asleep and I feel this tiny hand on my face and then there's a kiss on my forehead. And for a second I'm confused, like — did the tiny one do that? He's only four weeks old? Is he a mutant? That would be amazing.

And then I realise it's my big baby and I pull him into my arms while still asleep and think *Oh, he's delicious.* But then he elbows me in the boob and says ˙JAY JUNGLE. MAMA˙ and I'm like *Ughhh nooo, you're not delicious at all. What is that smell?* And I tell him to be quiet and I cuddle him and he says ˙NO JAY JUNGLE˙, and he climbs onto my chest and it hurts so bad because my boobs are about to explode. And then I cuddle/smother him and spend the next 40 minutes or so (who knows how long it was — it felt like days) getting him to sleep. And then I got him to sleep and I got up and I went to the bathroom and I came back to this . . .

And I was like 'IT'S MY BED! WHY ARE YOU EVEN UPSIDE DOWN? WHY CANT I HAVE ONE SPACE THAT IS MY OWN? WHY ARE YOU ALMOST THREE AND YOU SLEEP WORSE THAN A NEWBORN? WHY IS THERE NEVER ANY ROOM FOR ME?'

And even though this was an internal scream, the little one woke up angrily demanding a feed.

While feeding on the floor I took a photo and I put it on Facebook and Twitter. And on Twitter I said 'sigh' because the parents on Twitter get it. And on Facebook I did a slightly longer comment because I was trying to be a bit light-hearted because . . . well, we will get there . . .

I wrote: 'How come it's my bed and there's never room for me in it?' Which you'll note is not 'SERIOUSLY. WHAT THE FUCK . . .' It was meant to be funny, a way for me to be like 'see?' without being like 'OMG KILL ME. SEE?' And then I got this message, which I bloody always do, from a friend's mum. It said: 'Be grateful for your boys. They will be adults before you know it and they won't want to sleep with you. You should enjoy this time.' And I was like OK, I hope I'm never so unstable that when my sons are in their twenties I want them sleeping with me. But aside from that — CAN YOU NOT?

I know the first thing I'm going to be told is 'People are just trying to be nice! They're trying to comfort you.' Yeah, yeah, but it's hard to be charitable when you've only had two hours' sleep. Here's the deal: trying to be helpful or not — it isn't. It isn't helpful. It's condescending, patronising and it's actually (without being melodramatic but maybe a bit melodramatic) dangerous.

Constantly telling parents 'Be grateful! Be grateful! One day they won't be shitting on you and you'll be like "OMG, I long for the days when I was covered in sour milk and diarrhoea!" So be grateful! You might be so exhausted that you're crying on the toilet but these are the best days of your life SO BE GRATEFUL' leads to those parents shutting down and never sharing how they truly feel. It leads to parents not having support networks. It leads to parents walking into parenthood without any idea of how hard some moments, some days, can be. It leads to such unfair expectations on parents — enjoy every minute or you're a monster. It leads to feeling like you're doing it all wrong.

I am so grateful for my kids. I can't even put into words how grateful I am. So I don't need you to tell me to be grateful. I am. Guess what — I can be so grateful and so tired. I can be so grateful and so fucking over it. I can be so grateful and also imagine temporarily not having kids and just pashing and dancing and drinking bourbon and Coke in a really irresponsible way.

These comments always come from people with grown-up kids. And I get it. Maybe. I mean, when the boys are in their twenties I might be wishing they still lived with me and needed me 24/7. I mean, I kind of hope in my late fifties I'll be acting like I am in my early twenties — getting frisky with their dad, drinking bourbon, going to gigs, spending all my money on band t-shirts and fast food.

But I digress . . . I get it, kind of. Your kids are grown, you miss them, you see parents at the beginning of their parenting journey and it makes you nostalgic. I get that there's no malicious intent.

But again — can you not? Because when I make a heavily sanitised comment about not sleeping and you make a comment about being grateful, it implies I'm not grateful. And in my sleep-deprived state it makes me feel like an asshole.

And this might seem like an overreaction to a comment, but I (and other parents) get it All. The. Time. The other week I said: 'Just as one little bogan falls asleep, another little bogan wakes up. They're like a tag team', and I got one comment and three messages with the 'one day you'll miss it/be grateful' message. I get it about once a week. And the more I get it, the more I feel like I can't talk about the hard parts of parenting, or the things I'm struggling with. Because I don't want to appear ungrateful for my awesome kids, even the one that hates sleeping. And you see how that's a problem, right?

So, here are some things you can say instead of 'be grateful':

* 'I don't remember how hard it was never sleeping because I'm retired and I sleep until 10 now and I spend all day playing Candy Crush. So I'm just going to shut the hell up.' (Might be too specific.)
* 'That sounds tough, want me to drop you over something with chocolate in it?'
* 'You don't look tired at all. You look like a glam actress who only eats paleo stuff and drinks grass smoothies.'
* 'I heard kids who don't sleep are smarter than kids who do.'
* 'Parenting is really hard sometimes. It's OK to find it hard sometimes.'

MOTHERS AND BABIES

They say you'll move mountains, one day you'll change the world . . . that you have so much potential. One day.

But you've already changed the world. My world. You've moved mountains to me. You're already so much.

When I held you in my arms for the first time — you opened your eyes and looked at me. And you changed my world.

To me. You're everything. Already.

Every baby changes the world by being.

They make mothers. And mothers change the world, too.

THE NIGHTMARE OF NOT SLEEPING

Someone told me once that if you lie still at night and just breathe quietly it's the same as being asleep even if you can't sleep.

That person was full of fucking shit.

The thoughts I have at midnight — and 2 a.m., and 2.30 a.m., and 3.45 a.m., and 4 a.m., and 5 a.m., when usually I drag my bone-tired and weary ass out of bed — are not relaxing or even any concepts similar to relaxing.

Here is a not exhaustive (just exhausted) list of things I think during the night as I am rocking and shushing the baby back to sleep.

OTHER PEOPLE ARE AWAKE RIGHT NOW

I think this because I cannot cope with the idea that everyone is enjoying a beautiful, restful slumber except me. Somewhere there is another mother just like me, and she's hunched over a baby and she's whisper-cursing through gritted teeth and trying to get her baby to sleep. Somewhere there's another mother who is listening to her partner's snoring and trying to work out what the maximum sentence for murder is in this country. Somewhere there's another mother who is trying not to cry because she just got her baby to sleep and she knows they'll be awake on the next cycle but her heart is racing because she's now under too much pressure to sleep.

I cannot think about the mothers who are asleep and whose babies are asleep. It's too much.

Everyone should be awake and miserable because I am.

I AM NOT A NICE PERSON

My thought process here basically follows on from angrily spiting unknown mothers whose children sleep and then feeling really guilty about that because I like other mums and I know sleep is only one aspect of parenting and they're just lucky. Our babies might have been born on the same day, under the same sky (not in a field, but you know what I mean) and they might have opened their eyes to the world at the same exact second — and one sleeps and the other doesn't. And that is life. And I must be a not-nice person to think ill of mothers who are just lucky as I am unlucky.

And then I think — I am very tired and not very rational so I should give myself a break. But also, WHY THE FUCK WON'T MY BABY SLEEP WHEN THEIR BABY SLEEPS 80 MILLION FUCKING HOURS AND MINE NEVER FUCKING SLEEPS IT IS NOT FUCKING FAIR.

And then I think — hey, you sound like a not-nice person.

And then I tell myself to fuck off, I am a nice person, I'm just tired.

And then I have a fight with myself.

And then I think maybe I'm going crazy because I just yelled at myself in my head.

And then the baby wakes up and I think: *Jason Momoa in a loin cloth picking me up and carrying me into a cave and then there is a rock fall and we are stuck in the cave for all of winter and there is only one way to keep warm . . .*

And I pat and shush the baby and I think about my Jason Momoa Cave Rock Fall *Oh, I forgot my lighter, we can't have a fire, whatever shall we do to keep warm?* fantasy which keeps me calm and centred and actually it's my meditation.

Jason Momoa Cave is my happy place when I know it's almost morning and my oldest will be up soon and the day will start and it's so overwhelming and how am I going to get through the day when I am already so exhausted and what if not sleeping is actually damaging the baby's brain and I can't believe I wasted money on a fucking sleep consultant and I am doing all the things they said to do and nothing works and and and and

There are animal-skin rugs in the cave. And it's a very clean cave actually, and I brought my iPod and speakers so we can listen to some Nick Cave . . .

And I drift off to sleep in Jason Momoa Cave land and then suddenly the baby screams and I'm awake, I'm awake, I'm . . .

BABIES THAT WAKE OFTEN ARE SMARTER

I read a study that said this, and I one hundred per cent believe the study because I want to. Never mind that I ignore every other study. I believe this one.

I will have a smart baby.

He will probably cure cancer or work out how to get reception on the downstairs TV or something truly amazing that will benefit the world or at least me because I want to watch TV downstairs sometimes so I don't have to always watch *Deep Sea Alaska Crayfish Fishing Gold Hunters* or whatever hillbilly hunting weirdo reality TV my husband is always watching.

I will have a smart baby.

He will probably cause me no trouble ever because he will problem-solve and be clever and help his classmates at school and teachers will love him and they'll say to me, 'He's amazing! Did you teach him all he knows?'

And I'll say yes.

And it will be a lie but they won't know.

And I'll think, yes, it was worth waking 8346729 times a

night for 18 months to have a prodigy. Not every child can be a genius.

But mine can.

And I'll drift off to sleep imagining him thanking me when he wins a Nobel Peace Prize and then I'll wake again to screaming and then . . .

I WILL WANT TO GIVE UP

The last wake-up of the night is always the one when you think — *I just can't. I can't do this anymore. It's too hard. This is torture.*

The last wake-up of the night is the one where your eyes struggle to even open because your body is saying NO MORE. NO MORE.

And your head is thumping and you want to cry and it physically hurts.

And you'll hold your baby to your chest just a little bit tight but you'll feel their body soften in your arms and you'll think:

This is why I keep waking up to you. You need me. Now. Just now. I want to give up but I can't and I won't because you need me.

And it's OK to feel so overwhelmed by that need.

But when their breathing grows calm, when their head feels heavy on your shoulder, when their fingers gripping your arm soften, when they're finally asleep again, know this:

You wanted to give up but you didn't. And you're still here. And you helped them get to sleep because they can't do it on their own.

And there are mothers everywhere doing this, too, and you're part of a secret sisterhood of no sleep.

And you are wrong when you think you're a not-nice person because lack of sleep has frayed your edges. To your baby you're home and the nicest, snuggliest home there is.

And girl, you deserve Jason Momoa Cave action, and though he's probably married or something I bet he would be up for it if he was single and for some reason in your bedroom in the middle of the night because he would be super-impressed by your ability to get your baby back to sleep.

And your baby will be really smart and do wonderful things because they're your baby and of course they will.

And you didn't give up.

You didn't.

As the sun rises, and you need to take a deep and heavy breath to greet the day, give yourself a pep talk.

Namaste the shit out of this day. Hashtag blessed the whole bloody morning.

Down a cup of coffee.

Look the day in the eye and say: I'm ready.

If you can get through 8346729 wake-ups in a night there is nothing you can't do.

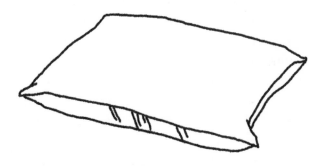

GLOWING

About three seconds after I had my second child, somebody said, 'Do you miss being pregnant?' and I thought — *Awww, that's cute.*

I smiled and said no, but I could have provided a list of all of the things I prefer to being pregnant. It's a short list:

Anything.

There are a few magical women out there who have amazingly easy, symptom-free pregnancies. These women are rare beings. I have met two. One of them, when drunk (well after the baby had exited the womb) admitted it wasn't that great. 'It was kind of OK some days, and then other days I wanted to die a little bit.' Oh, alcohol! So good for honesty.

I was *so excited* about getting pregnant. I cannot even tell you. I basically spent half of my life imagining myself as a pregnant woman. Daydreaming about being pregnant was a full-time preoccupation for me for around four years. It was a painful time, too. So many negative pregnancy tests, so many tears. I vowed I would never be one of those ungrateful women who complains about being pregnant. When I got pregnant I would enjoy it. Every second. And I *was* beyond grateful when I finally got that positive test.

My fantasy didn't just cover how I would feel (grateful, constantly ecstatic, blissful, at peace with my place in the world). The How I Would Be When I'm Pregnant fantasy covered everything: I would be me, with a beautiful bump, glowing (obviously), just kind of quietly amazing, you know? I'd wear floaty dresses — gorgeous ones. In my fantasy I wore a lot of chiffon and I frolicked in fields of lavender. I'd have glossy hair — I *knew* pregnancy gave you beautiful hair. I might feel nauseous — but just enough in the early stages to make sure the baby was healthy. You know, just enough to be able to say, 'Oh yeah, I do have a bit of morning sickness.' I'd be uncomfortable, sure. But not like really uncomfortable. It's only the last week or so that you're really uncomfortable, right?

Well, it wasn't quite like that. Not quite.

Pregnancy was difficult. Hahaha, actually let me rephrase that: PREGNANCY WAS HELL ON EARTH LIKE ACTUALLY THE WORST THING I'VE EVER BEEN THROUGH IN MY ENTIRE LIFE AND ALL OTHER LIVES I HAVE LIVED EVEN THOUGH I DONT ACTUALLY BELIEVE IN PAST LIVES BUT PREGNANCY WAS SO BAD I THOUGHT MAYBE THERE WERE PAST LIVES AND I HAD KILLED LOTS OF INNOCENT PEOPLE AND THIS WAS MY PAYBACK BECAUSE WHAT COULD I HAVE DONE TO MAKE MY LIFE SO INTOLERABLE FOR 37 EXCRUCIATING WEEKS?

A little nausea, you say?

I puked every single day of my first pregnancy, including on the way to the hospital to give birth. I once puked in the sacred waters of the Court of Appeal on my way to work (I'm sorry, New Zealand). I slept holding a bowl so that when I woke up during the night to vomit I wouldn't vomit in bed (again). I lost so much weight in my first trimester that I got used to people saying, 'What's your secret? You look amazing!'

Here's my secret — vomit so much that you are scared you actually spewed out some of your insides and you yell out to your husband that you need him to check your puke because you're worried your gall bladder is in there.

You think that's gross? I haven't even said the word *discharge*.

I vomited until my throat bled. My gums swelled. I felt so weak that my husband had to help me into the car in the mornings and after work. As we drove to work I'd vomit into an ice-cream container. I could barely keep down water.

Things improved, though, and by the middle of my second

trimester I was puking only twice a day and once or twice overnight. Bliss.

My hair? It fell out. Basically I was malnourished so I had clumps of hair falling out. It was awesome.

I was huge. Like a whale ate a whale. I had imagined a cute little bump but I was basically needing a wheelbarrow to get my massive bump around from 25 weeks.

When I slept it was more blacking out from lack of energy, so insomnia wasn't really that much of a problem until 30 weeks. People are really helpful about insomnia in pregnancy.

'Sleep now! Soon you won't be getting any sleep!'

Oh, thanks! So helpful! I'll just tell myself to sleep and then I'll sleep. And reminding me when I'm exhausted that I'm going to be more exhausted? Wow, thank you! That's not something a sadist would say at all!

You think this is bad? Wait until death!

To be honest, I got more sleep *after* the baby was born. I wasn't peeing every eight seconds for a start. For the whole second half of pregnancy you basically pee and then you pee again and then you're like, I definitely can't pee more, but you pee once more. And then the effort of standing up from the toilet makes you pee.

I'm a lady so I'm not going to talk about poop. (That part was bad.)

To help you with all of this amazing joyous joy, you have lots of people telling you how to be pregnant. Frankly, I enjoyed crapping more than I enjoyed the endless advice:

Have you tried ginger? *Yes, it made my vomit smell like ginger.*

Have you tried yoga? *Yes, it really helped me vomit in a new place.*

Have you tried highly concentrated bull semen? *No. No, I am not interested in semen of any kind right now.*

Or it's just random statements that you didn't ask for:

The vomiting stops after the first trimester. *Cool. I'm 28 weeks. How does it feel to be evil?*

It's not that bad, I did it five times! *OK, but I'm not sure what your poor life choices have to do with me.*

Just enjoy it! *OK, since you said that, I will!*

Pregnancy is a miracle. You should feel blessed. *I feel bloated. Go away before I stab you.*

You're lucky, you know. *Yes, I know that. I know. But thank you for making me feel worse than I already do. That is really nice of you.*

Don't even get me started about people touching you.

I felt like I wasn't just carrying a baby — I was carrying 10 pounds of pure rage. Everything made me angry. Once a colleague put the milk back into the work fridge with only a tiny bit left in it and I had to walk around the building because I was worried I might actually physically hurt him.

Emotionally I was wrecked, too. I was constantly terrified I'd lose the baby. Every time I went to the toilet I looked down at my underwear in terror — would there be blood? This never stopped. Even in labour I worried the baby would be stillborn. I worried when the baby didn't move. I worried when it did. I worried that my worry would make the baby sick. Every scan I could barely look at the screen.

I felt guilty all of the time. I should be loving this! I'd wanted this! I had been desperate to be pregnant. We had tried for so long. Why couldn't I enjoy it? What was wrong with me? Why wasn't I trying hard enough to just 'go with the flow'? To just 'embrace' being with child? To celebrate this special time? Did everyone else hate being pregnant?

I kept being told it was such a short time. That it would be over and I'd miss it.

And you know what? They were right.

Nah, just joking. They were full of it. I didn't miss it at all.

I willed that sucker (I mean my beloved first-born) out of me by sheer hatred of being pregnant. Come 37 weeks I just went *no more*. And my Eddie was born. I just needed to not be pregnant anymore. He knew. I knew. My body knew. It was all over.

And I didn't miss it at all. I'd never been happier than when I held him in my arms because 1. I wasn't pregnant anymore and 2. he was here, and safe.

I vowed I would never, ever, ever do it again. But I am not a smart person. And everyone said it would be different the second time. So I thought . . . yes, it will be different. It's totally worth it for the baby so maybe I should try again. The second pregnancy won't be the same. It won't be easy, but it might be easier.

And I was right!

No, I wasn't. It was terrible. Even worse than the first time. Except this time I took anti-nausea medication, which I recommend. First time around I didn't because I was a martyr or something.

Anyway — the one thing I learned from all of that is this:

Nothing. I didn't learn anything. I mean, I did it again! I would do it again! Ridiculous! So don't listen to me. I don't know what the hell I'm talking about.

Oh wait — actually I do have a message. I changed my mind. My message is this:

It's OK to hate it. It's OK to hate being pregnant. Pregnancy sucks. I mean, it's a miracle or whatever but it's also awful. And you're not a bad mother for hating it. For wishing it was over. You're wishing for an end to the horrible parts of it, not your baby. That's OK! That's a totally understandable reaction! It's OK to want it to be over. That's normal. If you're in pain, if you're sick, if you are exhausted — it's perfectly normal to not want to be. Think about it — if someone said they were really sick, would you tell them to suck it up because they're alive, so whatever? No, you wouldn't. So be nice to yourself. Beating yourself up makes everything worse.

You don't have to enjoy it. How you react to pregnancy doesn't have any impact on what type of parent you'll be. I was an awful pregnant person. I am an OK, sometimes quite good parent.

Don't let people make you feel guilty. Ignore garbage advice (including this if it doesn't ring true for you). Don't listen when friends or family tell you how great it was for them — they probably don't remember how terrible it was. Your baby will be born and that will be the amazing bit.

It's OK to hate every second of your pregnancy — it won't mean a thing when you hold your baby in your arms.

That's the best bit.

FIRST BIRTH —
SHOCK AND AWE

If I were to use one word to describe my first baby's birth it would be 'shock'.

My contractions had started on the Friday night then slowed during the day on Saturday. I went into hospital on Saturday night, and he was born at seven in the morning on Sunday.

In the final stages, I remember screaming for my husband to call a midwife: 'He's coming out right now!' The midwife said I needed to calm down and that my baby was a wee way off. I think the look of absolute terror and alarm on my face made her reconsider and she quickly checked me. 'Oh, he's coming right now!' she said rather cheerily. Far too cheerily than was needed, considering my vagina was on fire.

'IS IT TOO LATE FOR AN EPIDURAL?' I screamed.

And then suddenly he was here. Writing this three years on, and after the birth of my second son — *he of the enormous head and no pain relief* — I'm sure I've glossed over . . . umm . . . everything. I'm sure it wasn't quick. But I do remember the suddenness of it. I don't really remember the pain of that birth, and I know it was a good one as far as births go.

That's why I decided to get a photographer for my second birth. I thought it would be really, really zen, because I'd managed my first birth without too much drama.

Oh, I was a fool. No two births are alike. And I was just lucky the first time around. I had a six-pounder. In the right place and ready to go. I've learned (painfully, very bloody painfully) that that's very different to delivering a 10-pounder the wrong way around with a head the size of a basketball.

But I do remember the shock. Suddenly I was holding a baby in my arms. I was shaking with adrenaline and I tried to steady myself. Instinctively I wanted to hold him tightly to my bare chest. I had protected him for so long, dreamed of his face for even longer, and now he was here.

My baby.

There's nothing like those first few moments. It's indescribable (though clearly I'm going to try to describe it). I was exhausted, exhilarated. I felt like I could take on the world — though I didn't want to, of course, I just wanted somebody to sort out the searing pain below my waist.

I stared at my new son, utterly entranced. I remember my husband saying 'my son' and the words felt like dawn shining through a curtain, the break of day, a brand-new beginning.

He was quickly taken from me and given to my husband as they worked to patch up my decimated downstairs area (this is absolutely the politest way I can describe the horror). While I gazed at my husband, who was now trembling, with big, fat tears silently falling down his face, I could feel this utterly overwhelming joy and love for my child sweeping over me.

It filled the spaces all around my utter shock at suddenly becoming a mother. You have about eight months (if you're lucky and find out straight away) to prepare to be a parent. Less time (more time?), I imagine, if you adopt. But while you generally have time, you can't prepare for that moment.

You prepare the nursery. Buy far too many onesies in the wrong size. You buy little hooks to hang little coats. You buy those little shoes that you'll never actually use because they're always super-impractical and the wrong size. But this is how you think you're preparing.

And obviously it's important, we do need to prepare the practical things. Lay out the soft blankets in the cot, put the baby monitor together, buy the pram and the baby carrier . . .

But you can't prepare your heart. You can't prepare your heart for that seismic shift.

When I held him in my arms, the love I had for him filled every little space. Seeing my husband hold him and become a dad before my eyes, the love in the room threatened to overwhelm me.

The shock was enveloped by a rushing river of all of the love I've ever given or have ever been given in this life.

I know not every parent has that moment then, so soon after birth. Others will find it weeks or maybe months down the line. But you have that moment where you suddenly realise you've been given this important and incredible job — to love with all of your being. This capacity for love is a beautiful thing. It is so precious.

And I think that's why for so long after the birth you have these moments when you think — *I am a mother!! I am somebody's mother!! His!!*

And you bloom in this love, in this new role, even when it's impossibly hard.

It is that love that will sustain us always — the agony of no sleep for months or even years on end, the anxiety over the best way to handle a problem when caring for your wee one, the crushing pain of seeing your child hurting and not being able to take it away from them.

Love like a river, just like when you first really saw them. Just like the first time you knew this was your baby.

The shock edges away quickly. The gentle routines begin. That ordinary day-to-day dull wonder of life with a newborn takes over. But the love is ever-present — like water lapping around our ankles.

Reminding us it's always there — we love and we are loved. What a gift, what a job.

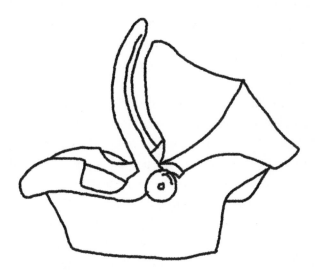

BIRTH #2

I'm not sure where to begin when it comes to my second child's birth. I suppose I should begin with the absolutely bat-shit ridiculous expectations I had about his birth. Eddie's had been relatively straightforward. I stupidly assumed a second baby would be easier than the first. Because Eddie's was quick, I figured I would basically cough and baby number two would come out.

Because I'd managed without an epidural the first time, I figured I could do the same second time around, and go even crunchier with a home birth. *Ha ha ha.* As I said, there's a big difference between a baby facing the right way, in the right place, that's only six pounds and a baby that's facing up, isn't in the right place and is huge.

I was a massive, insufferable dick throughout my second pregnancy — although thankfully I was only a dick in my head. I kept telling myself, 'Please, this will be a piece of piss. Just chill for a while when you get the first contractions and hang out at home. The baby might even come before the midwife gets here.'

I had images in my head of just gently pushing the baby out (hahahaha 'gently') and placing him on my chest and then my husband being like, 'OK, she's had the baby' to the midwife by phone. In this fantasy Eddie didn't even wake up until the morning. He then climbed into bed with us and we all snuggled.

So utterly convinced I was that my birth would be a breeze that I booked a birth photographer. I *love* birth photos. You know, those ones in a pool where the mother looks all blissed out? I was like yes, please. I'll have that photo, thanks.

Needless to say, it didn't go down that way. At 35 weeks I had contractions after seeing the midwife. And they were agony. Leaving the midwife's office I almost squatted on Dixon Street. Luckily it's Wellington, so nobody gave me a second glance. My husband was hissing, 'What are you doing? Stop squatting in the street! Jeeeez!' and then Eddie was squatting next to me saying, 'Whatchoo do dear Mama?'

I got into the car and said, 'I'm having it. Call the midwife!' My husband was like 'Hold on, we were just in there, how painful is it? Can we just walk back over?'

And I was like:

So we rang the midwife and she told us to head to the hospital and she'd meet us there. On the way I tried not to scream because Eddie was in the car. Eddie kept rubbing my back and saying 'Sokay my darling! SOKAY DEAR MAMA! You alright dear Mama?'

When we got to the labour unit he was quite stressed, and when reception asked for my name he said 'Mama'. I settled in and my husband took Eddie home.

I started to think, 'This is good. I don't have to be pregnant anymore.' For some reason I never thought 35 weeks was too early. I had long thought I was a few weeks ahead and I'd had heaps of scans that suggested the baby was big.

I asked for the birthing pool to be filled and my midwife explained that because baby was coming early I would need to stay in bed. I was distraught at this. Apparently it's only after 37 weeks that you *don't* have to be strapped to a bed. So six hours later, I was actually kind of happy that the contractions stopped. I went home. I was put on bed-rest. Goal: make it to 37 weeks.

The next night — the contractions started up again. They lasted about four hours at about eight to six minutes apart.

The next night they started up again. For about six hours.

It was the same night after night for a week.

I had no idea that this could happen. Eddie's birth had been straightforward. I'd had a contraction, then another one, they got closer together, then baby.

I had an exam and I was two centimetres dilated. I did not react well.

✪

I asked for a stretch and sweep and began to Google 'How to get a baby out'. I knew I didn't want an induction, and that since my waters hadn't broken I wouldn't get one anyway. So I ate 1500 pineapples, so much curry I never want to eat curry again, had exceptionally joyless sex (I'm sorry, husband, for being so aggressive) and I walked the streets.

The contractions were awful. I felt so alone. How do you say you're in labour but you're not in labour? I got all these comments like 'Can't you just get an induction?' or worse: people assuming I wasn't in labour because they didn't know you can be in labour for weeks . . .

Eddie took to pacing around the house, one hand on his back, groaning.

I laugh now, but it was pretty terrible at the time. I threw up constantly, couldn't pick up Eddie, couldn't do anything but lie in bed. A walk around the street exhausted me. I couldn't sleep. I could barely eat.

We ended up back in the delivery suite again a week and a half later, but I was only 3 centimetres. I was offered pethidine to help me sleep but instead decided to go home. I was distraught — if I was in this much pain now, I'd never be able to handle actual labour. This baby wasn't coming.

At 37.5 weeks I was still having contractions all night and part of the day. I picked up a birth pool from a friend on Twitter who was also a midwife. I needed something other than Panadol to take the pain away.

I set up the pool in my room in front of the TV and spent seven hours in there and in the shower.

My contractions were close together and it was agony. I began screaming and losing it, so we called the midwife — 'we', as in my husband, rang and said 'I think the baby is coming or something' while in the background I emerged from the pool screaming.

The midwife told us to go into the hospital. I had this exchange with the father of my child:

'CHANGE YOUR TOP!'

'What? Is it dirty?'

'CHANGE IT!'

'Why?'

'I CANT HAVE SKULLS IN THE DELIVERRRRAGGGHHHHHHHHHHHHHH'

changes top to a singlet

'WHY ARE YOU WEARING A SINGLET AND A HAT AND SUNGLASSES ITS NIGHTIIIIIIIIIIIIIMMMMAAARRRRRRGGGGGHHHHFFFFFUUUUUUUUUUUUUUUUUUCCCCCKKK YOoooooooooooooooooo0000Oooooo00oooooouuuuUUUUUUUUUU!'

We got into the car and began driving to the hospital, which involved me screaming at him to drive faster and him saying we needed to drive to the speed limit. We hit every red light on the way. At one point this guy pulled up next to us eating KFC and he turns and looks at me in the car and I'm like:

He almost dropped his chicken wing.

The contractions were so strong and I felt like I had to push. As we entered the hospital car park I basically jumped out of the moving car and screamed at a person trying to open their car 'GIVE ME AN EPIDURRAAAAAGGGHHHHHHHHH!' They flattened against the side of their car in terror, keys fumbling in trembling hands.

I banged on the glass doors at the hospital entrance, screaming at the top of my lungs as my husband sheepishly followed behind me. The bored security officer pressed the button and I lunged inside. 'IT'S COMING OUTTAAAARGHHH SHHHHHIIIIIIITTT!'

I hurried to the lift. I knew where to go as this was my third time in the hospital for this labour. The orderly in the lift looked like a character in a horror movie who is desperately trying to escape a serial killer. He frantically mashed at the lift buttons and tried to make himself as small as possible in the corner of the lift while I screamed, 'I NEED DRUGS! DRUUUUUUUUUGS!'

'Miss, I can only push the buttons on the lift,' he quivered in fear.

My husband suggested I calm down. I did not take it well.

When I finally got to the birthing suite my midwife heard my screaming and grunting and told me she wouldn't check me. She said if I felt like I needed to push I should push. And I really, really felt like I needed to push. So push I did. As hard as I could. While screaming for drugs.

After an hour or so (who knows, really? It felt like 8000 years) she checked me and I was only 4 centimetres. I was devastated. I don't think I've ever been so upset about anything in my entire life. I was sobbing, exhausted. How would I handle active labour if I was only 4 centimetres and in this much agony?

It was around 10 at night. I got into the pool and cried. At one point my midwife told me, 'You know this baby is going to come out, right?' It sounds so bizarre but I really didn't think the baby *was* coming out. I actually thought I might be in labour forever. I had hoped that when I had finally got to hospital and begun to push that it would finally be easy.

I still had the overwhelming urge to push, but there was no baby. The baby was posterior and pressing down on an anterior cervical lip (or something, I don't even know, but there was something about a cervical lip and it was anterior). He was facing up instead of down. Grinding against my pelvic bone. That was behind my need to push, and also why he wasn't coming out.

The only upside was that he was never in distress. He was happy as a clam through the whole process. From 35 weeks until his birth at 37.5 weeks.

My midwife was so calm. And the calmness helped me even as I felt totally at sea. I was in *agony*. And felt that the baby just wasn't coming.

I showered for a while, but kept grunting and trying to push out the baby. I felt like my spine was being crushed. I just cannot describe the pain. General things I said over the next five hours:

* CUT IT OUT
* PLEASE. I NEED DRUGS

* I CAN'T DO IT (the main thing I said)
* I'M DYING. PLEASE
* I'M GOING TO DIE
* PLEASE PULL IT OUT. PLEASE
* WHY WON'T IT COME OUT?
* HELP ME (I said this heaps)

My midwife was calm and collected. If she was stressed, I didn't see it. She kept telling me how strong I was and reminding me that not only could I do it, I *was* doing it. The baby would be born, she said. I spent a lot of time apologising to her after yelling at her. I spent a lot of time whimpering that I was dying.

My husband was quite pale at this stage — he was in a fair bit of pain from me gripping his arm. But let's be clear: *it was nothing like my pain, OK? Not even close.*

I felt like I had to push again, so I got onto all fours. I pushed and pushed and pushed and pushed. I felt absolutely delirious with pain. Eddie's birth had not been painful like this — the pushing had been a fantastic relief from the contractions. This was beyond anything I'd ever experienced before. I begged for any kind of drug available. At one point I even said I would take experimental drugs. Just anything — whatever is left over next door. Just, like, punch me in the face or give me some plants from outside the hospital. Just, like, *anything.*

My husband stroked my hair and reminded me that my plan was for an unmedicated birth so that we could get home as soon as possible to be with Eddie. I told him that I hoped he died and went to hell and then died again just so he could be sent to hell again because he's a fucking monster.

For the next little while I pushed and screamed, 'Is he coming? Is he coming?' The midwife said something about 'I'm just going to get my hand and . . .' I just screamed 'PULL IT OUT JUST FUCKING PULL IT OUT' at her.

Now, I would love to say he just came out. But he did not. He *did not*. I felt his forehead. Then the ridge of his eyebrows. Then his nose. Then his chin. Then his shoulders. Then his arms. Then his bottom. I felt it all. Ring of fire? It was an inferno. The entire room was on fire.

When he was put on my chest, I lost it. I sobbed and sobbed. I've never felt such relief in my life. Just writing this I'm sobbing. *I did it.* I got him out! My husband kissed my forehead and I stared at my beautiful, ginormous, almost ten-pound baby.

He was screaming. He was bruised and red. His head was enormous and swollen and misshapen. I awkwardly asked if his head was going to stay like that. My midwife assured me it wouldn't.

She told me she was just going to have a look at my lady garden, which was now a tornado-destroyed, desolate wasteland. I hissed at her, YOU BETTER NUMB EVERYTHING FROM THE WAIST DOWN BEFORE YOU TOUCH ME. She prepared a needle and I relaxed into the bed, holding my screaming cone-head. 'Please sew my vagina up entirely. I will never use it again,' I told her.

As I lay there with my legs apart, I remembered the lovely birth photographer Jane was there. I'd completely forgotten about her. I quietly said to her, 'Please don't take photos of my butthole.' She assured me there would be no butthole photos.

My husband gazed adoringly at our little boy. 'Wow, he's perfect,' he said. I called my family and told them the wonderful news. Our gorgeous baby was here. We were four now.

We went home a few hours after he was born and climbed into bed together. I felt completely at peace. It was over. Finally. And now the real fun would begin . . .

My midwife's words hung in the air: 'You did wonderfully.' And it was wonderful. A wonderful world for our new baby to be born into.

The sun began to peek through the curtains. We cuddled. Wonderful.

DAY THREE

ℓℓℓℓ

After the horrific ordeal that was my second labour, my wonderful midwife came over for our first check. She weighed baby and did the usual midwife-type things and then she said as she left: 'Remember, around day three you'll suddenly feel very emotional. This is hormonal. And it's normal. Just be ready for it. If you start to feel out of control, just take a breath.'

I immediately forgot this advice while staring at my little bundle of perfection who had been born only eight hours or so earlier.

On the morning of Day Three I was feeling very smug. I still had that adrenaline-fuelled-happy-happy-thank-all-of-the-gods-I'm-not-pregnant-anymore-look-at-my-perfect-baby rush going on. I was dressed, which I felt was a huge achievement. I was still feeling powerful (but in an *I survived a massacre* kind of way) about my son's birth. A coffee was all I needed and my day would be perfect.

I turned on my new coffee machine.

The little light with the beautiful little outline of a coffee cup didn't turn on.

What?

I pressed it again, but the little light with the little outline of a coffee cup didn't turn on.

I shook the machine. The light. It didn't turn on.

I took the thing out of the thing. It didn't turn on.

I hit the machine. It didn't turn on.

Suddenly I knew with every fibre of my being that this was my husband's fault. He had clearly broken the machine. Never mind that he doesn't drink coffee. That was a minor detail. I bet he fucking broke it and didn't fucking fix it. Probably *because* he doesn't drink coffee. You just can't trust people who don't drink coffee, even if you're married to them.

Then, like a deer about to be hit by a truck fuelled not by petrol but by pure incandescent rage, my husband walked nonchalantly into the kitchen.

'The coffee machine won't work. You need to fix it,' I told him.

'Can you just have a coffee at my mum's?' he said in a perfectly reasonable tone. 'We are already late.'

'HOW DARE YOU. HOW VERY DARE YOU!' I screeched. 'FIRST YOU GET ME PREGNANT. AND THEN YOU DENY ME COFFEE. YOU MONSTER!'

My husband blinked at me. 'Don't you think you're over-reacting a bit? It's just coffee. Just have one at Mum's.'

'JUST COFFEE? JUST. COFFEE. WHO EVEN ARE YOU?'

I launched into a 45-minute attack that covered most of his suddenly apparently numerous failings and the fact that there's only instant coffee at his mum's. 'Why can't you just fix the machine that you broke so I can just have the one thing I need in this world?'

Clearly our marriage was in trouble if he couldn't do this one thing that would make me so happy. Suddenly I was devastated. I had always thought we had a good marriage. People had commented on how good our marriage was. And now, it was all a lie. We would probably need to divorce. What kind of impact would this have on Christmas? I don't want to have to drive on Christmas Day when Christmas Day is clearly a day for drinking too much. What if he got a girlfriend? What if he married someone else? What if my new baby called her Mum?

He picked up the nappy bag.

'Are you leaving me?' I cried.

He stared at me, utterly bewildered.

I began sobbing.

I was clearly a terrible wife. I adored him. And I didn't want to raise two kids on my own. I didn't want my kids being raised by some other woman who would probably be far more attractive than me. *But he did break the coffee machine.*

'Umm, I don't know what's going on here but I think we should just go to Mum's and we can buy you a proper coffee on the way there.'

We cannot afford a proper coffee, I thought. We are so broke. What are we going to do? Now I have no coffee machine. I can't buy coffee and I can't make coffee at home. I'll have to go back to work tomorrow even though it's Sunday and the office will be closed. I won't be able to bond with my baby. He will turn into a serial killer. I'm going to ruin my precious baby's life. I fell to the kitchen floor, sobbing.

'I am a terrible mother,' I wailed. 'Just leave. Take the kids. They're better off without me.'

My husband stared at me with a look of confused fear on his face. He walked slowly over to the coffee machine, trying to avoid turning his back to me. He maintained eye contact. His movements were slow and deliberate.

He turned the power on at the wall. He pressed the button. The little light with the little outline of the coffee cup turned on.

THANK YOU

I said goodbye to my midwife last week.

I remember my excitement when I first heard her voice on the end of the phone. I was pregnant. Finally! My husband and I were absolutely ecstatic and utterly terrified. We had gone to our GP to declare our good news. Our test had been positive the day we had decided to 'do' IVF, so we had seen them only the day before. It was so surreal.

My husband said, 'Aren't you going to do a test?' Our GP stared at him, bemused. 'Well, didn't you do a pregnancy test?' he asked.

I'd done five. I'd been buying them in bulk so I just kept peeing on them. Stick after stick. My husband stared, disbelieving, as every one showed two stripes.

'One means you're pregnant. You did five. So you're pregnant.'

I think we just didn't want to trust a stick. Or five sticks. I'd had four surgeries to treat endometriosis. My first was only two weeks after meeting my husband. We were 17 and 18. I was told then I would struggle to have kids. I went off contraception after my third surgery. I had scar tissue, a damaged fallopian tube and we wanted kids. I was 22. I got pregnant at 26.

They take photos of your insides when they go in during surgery, and you can request them afterwards. I put mine on the fridge. When people would peer at the photos and say 'Wow, what's that?', I took great delight in saying 'That's my uterus!'

I've always been an over-sharer.

Our GP said our first step was a dating scan and then,

provided that went well, we needed to find a midwife. The dating scan was important, our GP said, as we were at risk of ectopic pregnancy because of my medical history.

We needed to wait another two weeks for the scan. Our honeymoon was booked for the next day. We went on our honeymoon worried the whole time that our baby was in the wrong place (the nice way of referring to an ectopic pregnancy, I suppose). We decided we wouldn't get excited and instead would pretend I wasn't pregnant until we returned and had the scan.

My husband bought a onesie on the first day of the trip. I puked all over the floor of our fancy hotel room. I puked in our fancy hotel bed. We went down to the hotel lobby to have our buffet breakfast and I puked in a plant. I'm sorry for puking in a plant, hotel-I-won't-name.

I puked watching Lamb of God, Hell Yeah, Slipknot, Marilyn Manson, Gojira and System of a Down at Soundwave. My husband gazed lovingly at me the whole time. Every spew was a good sign, he said.

We had our dating scan a few hours after arriving back in New Zealand. We sobbed staring at the little eight-week dot. Our dot was in the right place.

We carried the picture around for weeks, insisting that it looked like us. The dot replaced my messed-up (but clearly not *that* messed-up) ovaries on the fridge.

We booked a midwife. Hearing her say 'Congratulations' down the phone was one of the most exciting moments of my life. It signalled so much. Our long-wanted journey had begun. It was real. Our midwife made it real.

I had a terrible pregnancy. But my midwife was always there with me. She cheered us on. She kept me excited even when I was exhausted and overwhelmed. She more than tolerated my tears of frustration in her office. She was more than my midwife, she was my counsellor, too.

I felt so guilty that I had wanted a baby for so long but absolutely hated pregnancy. I didn't feel in touch with my body. I felt unhealthy, exhausted, overwhelmed. I sure as hell wasn't glowing. But she was so patient and caring and gentle with me. She always made me feel like I was strong and gave me so much confidence. She never denied my feelings.

My midwife wasn't actually there for my first son's birth. It was her weekend off. But she'd built me up and made me feel brave so I wasn't scared when he came at 37 weeks.

The on-call midwife was lovely. I have never met a midwife who isn't a wonderful person. It seems to be a prerequisite. There must be something about the job that attracts selfless people.

In New Zealand we have an amazing system that includes post-partum support, so my midwife continued to visit for six weeks after my son was born. When he developed health complications she continued to support me for a further three weeks, helping me navigate that difficult world, before gently handing me over to a specialist team. She was always professional and I felt like she really cared about us.

I really feel that she set up my little whānau to prepare for all of the challenges that lay ahead. There is nothing more terrifying than having a sick child, but I had moments of calm in the dark of the hospital late at night when I thought of my midwife telling me I was strong and I could do this.

I swore I would never have another baby all the way through my first pregnancy, so I loved hearing my midwife's familiar laugh two years on when I rang her to say I was pregnant again. Again, my midwife was a rock. She shared my care with another midwife, whom I immediately fell in love with. She had tattoos and pink hair. I mean, Jesus: she was My People!

She helped me breastfeed, so she'll forever have a place in

my heart. Every time my little one hungrily gulps down milk I think of her. She also helped me when I started to really lose it from all the vomiting.

My second pregnancy took a huge emotional toll on me. The support I had from my midwives was everything during those months when I felt so out of it. They respected me. They were professional. Kind. Gentle. Caring. Compassionate.

My main midwife delivered my second boy and she was incredible. There's no way I would have made it through that labour and delivery without her incredible skill and support.

I've been cared for by five midwives over my two pregnancies, one for a delivery, another for a false alarm, another for another false alarm, and another as cover for my main midwife . . . and they've all been awesome, awesome people. I want to thank them all. I want to thank all of the midwives who care for us and bring our babies into the world. I want them always to have chocolate in their fridges and coffee in their pantries.

I said goodbye to my midwife last week and it broke my heart a little bit. I thanked her, of course, but my words weren't adequate. How can you ever thank someone enough for making you a family, twice?

My midwife made me a mother. I can never thank her enough.

SLEEP

If our household had a motto it would be: *Qui super omnia amatur somnus.*

Above all else, sleep.

Our coat of arms would be two pillows crossed over an unmade bed.

We are a home of two adults who have a deep and abiding passion and love for sleep, a toddler who seems to hate sleeping at night with the fire of a thousand suns, and a newborn who is learning to sleep.

In the night-time wars, what side will our newest human choose? Will he choose the light, and literally wake at 5 a.m. every morning to meet the sun just like our oldest did for an entire year? Will he choose his own bed? Will he choose sleep? Unaccompanied? At night?

Our toddler is convinced that at night Mummy and Daddy get out his trains and have raging 'Thomas-da-tank-asian' parties. He thinks we get out the playdough and make really cool stuff *for hours*. He thinks we play *Zoom Zoom Zoom We're Going To The Moon* on repeat while taking turns lifting each other up and spinning around at the lift-off part. If he sleeps, his patron saint Jay Laga'aia might turn up to personally sing him 'Rockabye Your Bear', and upon seeing him asleep promptly leave and never make another episode of *Jay's Jungle* or *Play School* again. So he must not sleep. Ever. And if he does, it must be with us. So that he knows we are not playing Matchbox cars without him.

He has an excellent sense of humour. When he stays at

Nanna's house (we love Nanna more than any one person could love any one thing), he puts himself to sleep at around 7 or 8 and sleeps in his own bloody bed for 13 bloody hours. We try to replicate the exact conditions but it does not ever (no, never) work. Short of moving in with her (which, surprisingly, she's not keen on), we can't get the same result.

She shows great sympathy for our predicament. She also never gives unsolicited advice. A kindness I will be thankful for for all of my sleepless eternity. After two years we don't need any more advice. But we still get it. Oh, do we get It.

I find the best way to cope with unsolicited, unwanted advice is to imagine stabbing the person giving it, repeatedly, in the face, thousands of times. It makes you smile, which releases endorphins, which stops you actually stabbing the person.

When they smugly mutter 'consistency is key' with their stupid smug mouth, I imagine them being eaten by a shark.

'Show him who is boss.'

'You need tough love.'

'Co-sleeping is the only way.'

'If you do that he will never leave your bed.'

'Use a night light.'

'Put amber beads in a blender and give it to him each night with a chaser of nightwishshade oil.'

'Draw a pentagram on the floor of your lounge, light eight candles and sacrifice a virgin on a full moon.'

Look, I promise you I've tried every type of ritualistic animal slaughter and worship of a deity there is — consistently. There are only so many virgin-blood cocktails I can drink.

So here's what we do, consistently. We do the only thing that feels right for this hopefully short-lived period of our lives — we choose sleep over all else.

Each night we kiss each other in the hallway and that kiss says the following:

I hope you get sleep but mostly I hope I get sleep. And whoever gets the most sleep will carry us through the next day and remind us that we are a family that loves each other very much.

Then we go off to the trenches with a stoic nod of the head. He, a broken man, climbs awkwardly into the bunk bed. I get the easier (some nights) option and climb into our bed and snuggle with our newborn (he's five weeks but I feel like he was born yesterday because there's been so little sleep in those five weeks).

This is the path of less resistance. The toddler isn't woken by the newborn. This is pacifism in action. If he wakes, he is comforted and settled by Daddy. If that means not sleeping in his own bed — so be it. Sleep — wherever it happens — is all that matters. It won't be forever, but it feels a bit like forever.

We meet in the morning, bleary-eyed. My husband makes me a coffee. I squeeze his shoulder and cover the toddler's face in smooches.

Our gorgeous, perfect firecracker of a child, who gives us so much joy every day, who is every single kind of adorable, my gentle, hilarious, sweet and spirited boy, beams up at me:

'Is morning Mama! I liddle sleeps! I seena jellyfush wif daddy. In my sleeps. WE GO BEESH? FOR SAN CARSULL? ON DA BEESH MAMA? FOR SAN CARSULL? SEEN A SHAAARK MAMA HAHAHAHAHAHA BEESH NAO MAMA? DADDY BEESH? THES A BEER UN DEEEEEA UNDA CHEEER US WULL DERA PEEPUL WEF GHEMS UNDA STORY TO TULL OPUN WHYYYYY CUMON SIIIIII IS PLAYSCHOOOO. BEESH MAMA? FOR JELLY FUSH? KINA KINA KINA KAI UN DA BASKUT . . .'

I catch my husband's eye and we try not to laugh. I start to make another coffee. One for the road.

We're going to the beach.

HOW TO WATCH A MOVIE WHEN YOU HAVE A BABY

Decide you want to watch a movie. Take 30 minutes to answer the question 'what movie shall we watch?' Forget what the question was because you're so tired. Take another 20 minutes trying to remember whether or not you've seen the movie that you're going to watch. At the most interesting part of the movie, the baby will wake up screaming. Pretend you don't hear it. Have a stand-off (sit-off?) with your partner as you both pretend you can't hear the baby screaming. Stop movie. One of you falls asleep on the couch while the other rocks the baby back to sleep. Eventually return 45 minutes later. Watch 10 more minutes of the film despite the fact that you can't remember anything that happened before the baby woke up. Look up Wikipedia page for movie. Baby starts crying. Kick partner off couch and then pretend it was an accident. Fall asleep while partner rocks baby to sleep. Tell coffee group the next day that you watched a movie.

THIS LONELY LIFE

eeee

There's so much about motherhood that I find lonely.

It's such a strange concept because you're almost never alone when you're a mother. You can't even poop without your little person handing you toilet paper. Showers have audiences. There's often more than two people in the bed and it's not the racy kind of more-than-two-people-in-a-bed experience. My two-year-old is always talking to me. 'Where's this? What's that? This please. That's mine! No! NO!' He provides a non-stop commentary throughout his day. All in the third person.

And yet — I feel deprived of conversation. I talk to him about why you have to be gentle with the 'beuful bufly' and why it's not a good idea to put rocks in the baby's basket. I talk to the baby: 'Are you hungry, sweetheart?' The answer is usually quite clear when he attacks my nipples with the ferociousness of an angry platypus (I imagine angry platypuses are very ferocious). I talk to myself: 'They're both asleep? At the same time? What do I do?'

I long to talk to other parents, while at the same time being too exhausted to actually engage in proper conversation with said parents or to seek out those parents to make said conversation. The internet helps. Writing has made me feel a lot less alone. Twitter was my lifeline when my oldest son was born, especially when I spent long nights awake in hospital staring at him with only my fears to keep me company.

Since I became a mother I have made some really, really great friends. Friends I can't imagine my life without now. I love them fiercely. They make life better. They're real friends where you know it's not just the kids keeping you together. When I went back to work I envied their playdates and wished I was sitting in their warm and loving homes sharing coffee. I missed them.

This — my second time around — is different, as they're all working or studying now. My home is warm and loving, but it's empty of adult companionship.

And at night, without my husband in bed with me, feeding in the darkness, I feel very lonely. There's something truly isolating about breastfeeding. Again, it's such a strange concept, because you literally have another being attached to you. But ultimately it's just you. You're alone with your sore, cracked nipples. That painful let-down that can be so forceful it can bring tears to your eyes in those early days. At a big family picnic on the weekend I sat in the bathroom, feeding. There's definitely nothing more isolating than hearing laughter and shouting when you're stuck in a tiny room alone.

I know I should go to playgroups. Maybe baby sensory group. Or a Rock 'n' Rhyme musical thing. There's a lot to do out there. But by the time I have the kids dressed and changed and fed, it's almost time for my toddler's nap. And I will not mess with my toddler's nap time. It's the only time I have to do any housework or to check the news or have a solo poop.

If I somehow do manage to get to one of the absurdly early mum-and-bub groups I feel so awkward walking in late with a toddler who is wearing a helmet, Batman cape and mismatched shoes. Especially when he's chomping on some not-organic-at-all, totally processed and definitely-bad-for-you type of food thing. I worry about what others are thinking. That's quite narcissistic because they probably don't give a shit. But I'm not a confident parent so those thoughts come easily.

I find mum groups intimidating. The other mums seem so together. They have philosophies — attachment parenting, free-range parenting, permissive parenting, evolutionary parenting, maybe even paleo parenting — like, no nuts or something. I can't even spell Montessori (I had to Google it). They speak with such confidence on positive parenting, body autonomy for children — all things I care about but don't feel I know anything about. What do you do if your parenting philosophy is just . . . try to make it through the day without anybody getting badly injured?

I'm sure my philosophy of Just Do Your Best and Love Your Kids is exactly the same as theirs when it comes to the crunch — but I feel overwhelmed with how onto it they are. They know what they're doing. Any topic there is, they seem to have thought a lot about how to approach it. I often just feel out of my depth.

Six weeks in, I'm lonely. So I'm going to have to sort it out.

Or I'm going to have to start a playgroup of mums who try hard but fail quite a bit but never intentionally. One where it's OK for me to show up with a bit of puke in my hair. Or to drink eight coffees even though I'm breastfeeding. Or to confess that I get Montessori and Steiner mixed up. One where it's OK to turn up late. And forget your kid's drink bottle. And wipes. Why do I always forget wipes?

Maybe I'll start recruiting today. Yes, that's what I'll do.

So, if a sloppy-looking, sweaty, haggard redhead with two kids hanging off her approaches you in the park — smile or run (depending on how you feel about what I've just said).

A PSA FROM
A CRANKY MUM

~~~

What Feels Like Everyone: 'Is he sleeping through the night yet?'

Me (through gritted teeth): 'He's doing great!'

Me (screaming in my head): *He's six weeks old!! What the fuck do you think? He's a newborn baby! Of course he's not sleeping through the night. Dick.*

WFLE: 'My cousin's baby slept through the night from just a few weeks old!'

Me (trying to restrain myself): 'That's truly something else. Your cousin is lucky!'

My internal scream: *Your cousin doesn't exist. Your cousin is full of shit or you are full of shit. Newborn babies are not expected to sleep through the night.*

WFLE: 'You should try sleep training. That's what she did.'

Me: 'I'm not worried. He's doing great.'

Losing my mind: HE WAS JUST BORN. *I hope you fall over and do something to your ankle. I hope it's sore for three days but not that sore that you can't work because I'm not that mean. I hope you get a really bad paper cut!*

✪

I know people are just trying to make conversation, but why are people so utterly obsessed with asking about how new babies are sleeping? I got asked if my littlest was sleeping through two days after he was born. *Two days!*

He's delicious. He smells like rainbows. He's the best thing I've ever done (along with my bigger baby). He smiles this gummy smile when he looks up at me. His hair is so soft. His cheeks are so fat. He is so perfect I want to have 10 of him. Who gives a rat's ass about whether he sleeps x hours at a time yet? He just got here. Just stare at him for a while. Welcome him! He's perfect, isn't he?

And to the people who *always* have to point out their sister's neighbour's ex-wife's cousin's baby slept through the night from eight hours old — wow, so awesome. That's a great thing to tell someone who is probably waking up every three to four hours if they're *very lucky*.

Or if your baby is one of those extremely, incredibly, exceptionally rare babies who slept for very long periods overnight from early on — how grand for you. Congratulations. Keep it to yourself.

Nobody who isn't sleeping needs to hear that you're sleeping, or that your friend's brother's aunty's mother is. Nobody.

Also, this fixation other people have on newborns sleeping through the night is why I thought my first-born would magically sleep through the night from eight weeks old. Lies! *Lies!*

Newborns aren't meant to sleep all night. They have to wake up for feeds. It sucks. Their mums are freakin' exhausted. So don't tell tales about sleep. Just look at how cute they are. And make Mum a coffee. She needs that more than talk about an imaginary baby who slept through from seven minutes old.

collapses into a heap

EVERYTHING IS RIGHT IN THE WORLD

There are times when you're asleep on your feet.

Your eyes hurt. Your jaw is tight and your back creaks. There's a mild but pounding ache between your ears.

And MUM MUM MUM snaps you back to reality. And then wailing. You scoop up your baby and they arch their back as they scream, their face red with fury. Clammy skin and fat tears.

You're so very, very tired. So exhausted that every part of you hurts.

Your nerves are fraying. You want to snap. You want to run. You feel desperately guilty for even thinking that.

And your screaming baby presses their tiny chubby fingers to your lips . . .

. . . and you pretend to bite them.

You nibble at them and say NOM NOM NOM.

Baby begins to giggle. Hesitantly at first. They pull their hand away. You make a chomp sound and go for them again. This time baby roars with laughter.

You are a mother.

Their mother.

You are their safe place.

Everything is right in the world.

I CRIED IN A PIE SHOP

Today was not a good day.

The day started at 2.30 a.m. It's never a good idea to start your day at 2.30 a.m.

The littlest one screamed in my ear. I was in a deep sleep. I was dreaming about Idris Elba. I did not want the things that were happening in that dream to end.

I put the baby on my boob and succumbed to the pain. It's always painful on that side. Sometimes I think my right breast is possessed. That's probably a sign that I'm not getting enough sleep.

Mercifully it is a quick feed. I can't be bothered putting the baby back in his cot. He somehow wasn't even in his cot anyway so I figure it's OK for him to keep snuggling into me. I haven't seen my husband in many, many years. I assume he is in the spare-room bed with our toddler.

I groggily stumble into the toilet and see a snake. It is huge. I lunge for the towel rail because I need to stop myself falling backward. I break the towel rail.

The snake is a towel. We do not have snakes in New Zealand. The baby wakes up.

I resettle the baby. My heart is racing. I'll check Facebook to calm myself. The first photo in my feed is a goddamn snake eating a goddamn croc.

My breast hurts so much I can't sleep anyway. So I just lie there imagining snakes. I try to turn them into fun snakes wearing top hats and getting upset because they don't have arms and their top hats keep falling down. It doesn't work.

Panadol doesn't take my boob pain away.

It's now 5 a.m. I write a post about how much I hate breastfeeding.

The baby wakes up. I feed the baby. It's now 6 a.m. I close my eyes.

At 7 a.m. my oldest comes in crying. He won't tell me what's wrong. My husband is looking for his work pants. He turns the shower on. I turn on *Play School*. The baby cries again. It must be a growth spurt.

We are all late. Husband says he has to go. He's sorry but he needs to get to this job. He cannot take our first-born to crèche because our first-born isn't dressed because he's watching *Play School*. I force myself into the shower. The oldest jabs my stomach. 'BABY INERE MAMA BABY INERE PUKU!' He laughs. 'Whasdat, Mama?' he says, pointing to my stretch marks. The baby begins to cry.

I put on a bra and immediately leak through it. I get another bra. I hear the bus. I am not on the bus. I am looking for underwear.

My oldest has smeared my moisturiser all over the mirror in his room. I ignore it. I make a coffee and hear the bus. I am not on it.

He begins his crèche half-day at 8.30 a.m. It's 9.30 a.m. I cannot find the baby carrier.

I cannot find my oldest son. I look out the window and see our gate is closed so I just sit down and feed the baby. I read the blog post I wrote about breastfeeding. It's crap.

I look for my oldest. He is filling a bucket with dirt and he has a hose in the bucket. He is filthy. I change him. The baby cries. I change my wet bra. We finally leave.

It's 10.30 a.m. I walk out just in time to see the bus leave without me on it. I begin to walk to crèche. It is so windy that I can barely hear my oldest screaming at me to STOP THE WIND. MAMA!

It's quite pleasant.

The baby cries. Could it be teeth?

I see another bus. I tear across the road, waving one hand while trying to steer the buggy with the other. The baby is laughing as he is bounced around in the carrier. My oldest yells 'FASTER. MAMA! FASTER!' from the buggy. The bus driver smiles at me and gets out of the bus to help me. 'Lovely kids you've got there,' he says. My oldest says 'HI! I'M EDDIE!'

I struggle to get the buggy brakes on. A young girl offers me her seat. I wave her away. She coos at my baby. 'What a cutie you are!' she says to him. He beams. Eddie says 'HI! I'M EDDIE!'

The bus driver gets up to help me off the bus. Before he can, an elderly woman leaps up and helps me with the nappy bag which has fallen out of the buggy and spilled shit everywhere.

The bus driver, the nana and the young girl wave and smile at me from the window as the bus leaves.

The baby actually spills shit all over me. I walk into the crèche and Eddie leaps out of the buggy. 'HI! I'M EDDIE!' he yells. His kaiako cheerily greet me. They help me with my bags. They pull up a chair for my boy. They pass me a glass of water. They pull out his lunchbox. I realise it's almost lunchtime. I say I need to go, and they say 'No worries! It's all good.' I rush out to the sound of my son crying. I bite back tears as my other son begins to cry. I watch the bus go past without me on it.

His kaiako rings me on my cell phone. 'I just thought you should know he stopped crying straight away. He's playing in the sandpit. Everything is OK.'

I walk home. It takes an hour and 15 minutes. I am sweaty and covered in baby poo. I get home and put the carrier in the washing machine. I put the baby in the sink.

After feeding the baby I realise I need to leave again to pick up the toddler. My husband comes home. He says he needed to get one of his tools. He drives me to crèche.

I stand at the door at crèche watching my son, who hasn't seen me yet. He is pretending to be a shark. He is screaming with laughter with the other children. He is covered in sand. He tells me he had SO MUCH FUN. I begin packing up his gear. The other mums smile kindly at me. 'Full-on day, eh?'

I grimace awkwardly at them.

The baby cries. I have squeezed him into a sling and he hates it. My sister rings and I accidentally hang up on her. My oldest screams at me to stop the wind again. I miss the bus. My sister calls again. I complain at her. I don't even ask her how she is. She asks for the boys' sizes so she can buy some clothes for them.

I remember I have someone coming round at 4 p.m. It's 3 p.m. The next bus is in half an hour. I go to the pie shop. I order a coffee. The lady offers to toast me a sandwich and gives me a warm smile. 'It's OK,' she says.

I think I didn't thank my sister on the phone. Did I thank the bus driver? That girl? The nana? My husband? The kaiako? The other mums? Every person who spoke to me today has treated me kindly.

My baby snores softly on my chest. My toddler sleeps in his buggy, exhausted from his exciting day. My husband calls.

'See you soon, hon. What a shitter of a day, eh?'

I nod. Hang up. And start to cry.

I cried in a pie shop. Because I'm thankful to everyone who is nice to mums who always miss buses.

HOW TO MAKE A MUM-FRIEND

Surely I'm not the only person who finds making mum-friends quite difficult?

I struck gold with my antenatal group, and three years on we are all really close. I have often wondered if it's rare — I feel like I was really lucky that they all ended up being really intelligent, chilled out, funny and fun. We are all on to our second babies now and don't get to hang out nearly as much as I'd like us to, due to work and life and illness. But we will always have a special bond because we had all of our boys (yes, all boys) together. We now have (almost) all had our second babies together as well — six boys, one more boy on the way, and one little girl.

I have another circle of mum-friends that I met online. There are big benefits to meeting mum-friends online — you know their politics, general outlook, ideological beliefs, etc *before* you get them into your house. I mean, sure, I have met a few people online who have ended up being creeps (who hasn't?), but thankfully I got them out of my life fairly quickly. My circle of online mum-friends (who, really, are just friends) is my lifeline. I adore them — they're my best friends. I don't know what I'd do without them.

I was pretty much the first in my circle of friends to have kids, so it means my mum-friend circles are just those two, really — my antenatal group and my friends I first met online.

Trying to meet mums in other ways is often a total failure. Someone will say something about 'natural' birth and I'll be all *lip curl* or they'll start talking about baby-led weaning or cloth nappies and two hours later I will come back and they will still be going so I'll go on a short holiday and then come back and they're just winding up and they have a book for me to read. And I just . . . why is it so hard? I'm not even that picky!

I feel like I have a script for meeting new mums, and it's like speed dating.

It always begins at the swings, eh? And the first question from either mum is almost always 'How old is yours?' Then there are comments about size of said baby — so big! So small! Testing the waters a little, there are questions about 'How do you find it with two?'

I always find these conversations so difficult. I feel so anxious all the time. So unsure of how to be cool for other mums or say the right thing or at least not say the wrong thing. After being inside all week I feel like I can't even make conversation. I mean, even at home I'm like CAN YOU NOT PUT IT IN YOUR MOUTH IF IT ISN'T FOOD. IS IT FOOD? NO. TAKE IT OUT. NOW. FOOD. MOUTH. NO FOOD. NO MOUTH.

If the other mum starts talking about the weather you know you don't have a chance. They're bored. You're boring. The conversation grinds to a halt. And Eddie is always awkward and refuses to get off the swings, so I have to just stand there.

Sometimes if the conversation actually seems to be going somewhere and I've managed to not say something really terrible like 'Yeah definitely, my vagina was super-sore afterwards', I will tentatively drop vaccination into the mix just to make sure I'm not putting in wasted effort.

I wish I was better at social activity. Just cool and smooth. Like that mum you see at the park with her latte and she looks really great and she's surrounded by other mums and they're all cackling. Heads flung back, beautiful Barbie hair shining in the sun, 'OH, JANA! YOU'RE TOO MUCH!' And she pulls out a hip flask and tells another amazing story and her perfect kids just sleep perfectly in their double buggy (one girl and one boy) and the buggy is one of those fancy ones that has the super-sweet black-and-white pattern on it.

I mean, I have mum-friends. It's just that all of us are at different stages — studying, working outside the home, that kind of thing. Those who are stay-at-home mums don't live near me, so we're not hanging out at the local park. And winter makes me anxious — there are germs everywhere. People take their kids out when they're sick. Everyone is coughing. It's cold. Winter really is a bullshit season.

So where is the anxious mums' club? We can all sit around and take turns being Janas. Have our moment in the sun. We can forgive each other for having verbal rotavirus (do you know, I once said to a person I only just met that I once puked in bed and slept in it because I was too sick to move. Who says that to someone? Over lunch? OMG, I just told all of you three people reading this. What is wrong with me?).

Where was I . . .? We would forgive each other's short attention spans and inability to keep on topic, going off on tangents and telling stories that don't go anywhere.

We can just be casual mum-friends who text and say 'going to the park want to come?' or 'mums and bubs movie at midday — keen?' I have friends who aren't mums that I can do this with, so I just wish I had more mum-friends, with kids the same age, who I could do this with.

And we can just see a movie. Or hang out by the swings. And not talk forever about boring 'parenting philosophies' or whose child is sleeping through the night or on solids or whose birth was the most natural (it was Jana's — she gave birth in a field with a paleo string quartet playing).

Maybe the trick to finding the right mum-friend is to

approach it like dating. Have a list of things that are non-negotiable.

So here are mine.

1. MUST LOVE MODERN MEDICINE AND VACCINATION.
My closest, dearest mum-friends know what I've been through with my son. They know modern medicine saved him. And they know the importance of vaccination.

2. MUST NOT TALK ABOUT SUPERFOODS. PARTICULARLY CHIA SEEDS. AND QUINOA. PREFERABLY NOT EVEN ABLE TO PRONOUNCE 'QUINOA'.
For a really long time I thought it was a fish and I called it kwin-oh-ah. The fact that so many people never corrected me really cranks my crank. Fuck quinoa. And superfoods. And conversations about food that aren't cake-related.

3. LIKES BEEFCAKES.
I would like my mum-friend to be someone who isn't unnerved by my obsession with The Rock, Idris Elba, Thor and, a recent return to my fantasies, Joe Manganiello. Also, the captain of the Samoan rugby team. And Roman Reigns. If this obsession can't be matched, I would at least like someone who enjoys spending a portion of their time talking about crushes.

4. THEIR CHILDREN MUST BE TERRIBLE SLEEPERS.
I just want to be with My People.

5. NO DIET TALK.
I don't want to feel bad about how I look. Particularly because I don't feel bad about how I look. Despite the fact that I think society wants me to feel bad about how I look.

6. WINE AND COFFEE — SOLID RELATIONSHIP NEEDED.

Yeah, I feel like my great loves in life are wine and coffee (and my kids and husband, I suppose, after wine and coffee). So if we have that in common that's going to be helpful.

7. GOOD POLITICS.

You don't have to agree with everything I do. But you kind of do.

8. MUST NOT MIND LISTS ENDING AT 8.

It's all a bit silly, I know. I think it's just winter. It makes you feel isolated. It's too cold to go out. The kids are always sick. When your child is finally better, your mum-friend's child is sick. So you just never get to hang. It sucks. Maybe I'm just being an emo.

But today I did meet a mum by the swing. I dropped a comment about vaccination and she said there should be a law requiring people to vaccinate. And then I dropped an F bomb just to see what would happen and she didn't even flinch. And then she said her almost-three-year-old still wakes up in the night. So . . . Wish me luck?

How long do I wait before I call her?!

PINTEREST-FAIL MUM

Sometimes when I want to feel bad about myself I go on Pinterest and look at what mums who have their shit together are doing.

I look at their miraculous messy play ideas at 3 a.m. and resolve to do them the next day with my toddler. My broken sleep is dominated by dreams of my son and me deliriously happy playing with home-made rainbow snow and glittery gloop and glow-in-the-dark playdough.

And then I wake up and reality hits.

'Shall we make some playdough?'

'No. No. I don' want dat playbo.'

'Come and make playdough with Mama! It'll be soooo much fun,' I say with forced cheeriness.

'No fun. No. Cars.'

I lovingly make the playdough while my son plays with his cars. He ignores my perky, sing-song commentary. He's probably thinking 'Who replaced my mum with this Stepford wife?'

I put glitter in the playdough. I follow the recipe to the letter, but the playdough is slimy. I add more flour. Now it is crumbly. I add more water. The glitter clumps together. It's both slimy and crumbly now. The recipe says it's fool-proof.

My son looks at the playdough, then at me.

'I don' like dat.'

I don't know who he's referring to. I chuck the playdough into the bin. I used an entire packet of flour.

⬤

I will make gloop. It has three ingredients. Surely I can't stuff this up.

I crush coloured chalk to make four bowls of gloop. All are different colours. My son is absolutely delighted. It has taken me all morning to make the gloop and get it to the right consistency.

'I like dat!'

I am ecstatic. Such praise! I run to grab the camera. It takes me three seconds.

I return to find the bowls of coloured goop upside-down on the concrete by the front door.

'Finish Mama. I finish da goop.'

⬤

I will make snow. The recipe says 'Easiest clean play recipe'.

I have decided that after spending two hours cleaning up after the eight-second gloop messy play I want to have clean play.

Three cups of baking soda. One cup of water.

It looks like snow. The toddler is excited. He begins to play with it and I think 'Good, I can empty the dishwasher.' I take one cup from the dishwasher and the toddler appears.

'Where's your snow?'

'I throwed dat snow away, Mama.'

He has tipped the bowl of snow from the deck onto the roof of the neighbour's house.

⬤

That night I don't dream of being a Pinterest mum. I look at the photos of the Pinterest mums and imagine them sneaking Valium and hiding vodka in their tea. Nobody can be that perfect.

In the morning a little voice says to me, 'Paint mine face,

Mama? Eddie paint mine mama's face?'

I look up 'home-made face paint'. I scan the recipe. I go to the shop and buy face paint instead. I know my abilities now. I know my shortcomings.

I put the different colours into a muffin tray. I Google 'face paint designs'. I look at the first website and read the instructions for 'butterfly'. I roll my eyes. Yeah, right. I turn off the computer.

I hand my son a paintbrush. 'Make Mama a butterfly,' I say.

He screeches with laughter as he paints my face. We get out a mirror and I paint his face as a 'butterfly', letting him instruct me on how to do it just right.

Afterwards we both look utterly ridiculous. We look into the mirror and he says, 'We beuful budderfies, Mama!'

Because we're on a roll, I grab the corn starch and pull the hose out. We grab a bucket and he grabs clumps of corn starch and chucks whole pieces of chalk into the bucket with the corn starch and then puts the hose in.

It makes an unholy mess and my little baker declares he is making GLOOP PIES! He then throws the gloop in the air because now he's making GLOOP PANCAKES!

We look like a Pinterest nightmare. And it's the most fun I've had in ages. His screams of laughter reverberate around the neighbourhood. And we play for two hours.

Perfection is overrated.

BEFORE I WAS HIS MUM

Oh, I was such a great parent before I had kids. I knew *exactly* how to parent.

I was a supermarket tutter (I would *never* give my child a Kinder Surprise just because they asked for it), I was a smirker on planes (I would *never* put a child on a plane late at night — I mean, you're just asking for trouble), I was an eye-roller over my latte (my child would be well behaved in cafés!).

And I was so breathtakingly wrong. I don't even know where to begin. Here are some of my dumbest pre-kid ideas:

NO SCREEN TIME FOR MY BABIES!

Don't you know? Screen time is The Worst. You may as well let your child play with broken glass covered in wasps. It'd be safer. Kids turn into zombies in front of the TV. Get them outside! Get them in *nature*.

Fuck nature. It's always fucking raining. The fact that TV turns kids into zombies for five seconds is the whole point. That's what you want, so you can make them a nourishing meal for them to throw on the floor.

Which brings me to my next dumb idea.

THEY'LL EAT WHAT THEY'RE GIVEN AND THEY'LL STAY AT THE TABLE UNTIL THEY'RE FINISHED!

I will not be pandering to my toddler. If he won't eat what has been made for him he'll go to bed hungry. He needs to learn that we are not his servants. I was forced to eat my veges, and he will, too.

We are his servants. He can eat whatever he wants as long as it's something. Because not eating means waking us up at 2 a.m. then 3 a.m. then 4 a.m. then 5.30 a.m. because he wants 600 grams of luncheon. Just luncheon. Nothing else. He wants the worst not-even-meat there is. He loves that crushed-up every-part-of-the-animal crap. It's better than cheese. Which he will also eat, if it's just cheese on its own.

Pre-kids, I knew how to deal with picky eaters — you force them to eat. Whatever is in front of them. Then they won't be picky.

Except that when you're actually staring at your child, you actually can't force them to eat because you realise how messed-up it is to force anyone to eat when they don't want to. Don't get me wrong, I've thought about it. And I once made him cry when in frustration I said 'For God's sake, JUST EAT!' Not my best parenting moment.

A stressed-out dinnertime is not what we want. He picks up on it, we feel like garbage and he doesn't eat. So now we don't push it.

When he's 30 he won't still be eating luncheon. In all seriousness, it feels like a long game. I don't want him to have messed-up attitudes towards food. We grow veges together as a family, and we cook them up and eat them — or he picks beans or cherry tomatoes straight from the garden and eats them raw. You win some, you lose some. Some weeks it's all plain rice crackers and cucumber. The next it's eating four out of the seven meals made for him.

Now, the next one is ridiculous:

I WANT THE LOUNGE TO STAY OURS.

I don't want us to be one of those houses where there's just toys and shit everywhere. The lounge is an adult space. I want a basket of toys (wooden, heuristic, just a few — kids don't really need many toys) that can be slid under a coffee table or something. Out of sight, out of mind. Then we can have time *not being parents*. You know, in the evening, after they go to bed at a reasonable time. We can have a glass of wine and toast what great parents we are.

Here's my lounge:

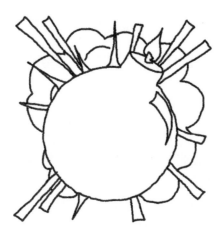

When the kids are finally in bed, we try to do a quick clean-up, which involves me throwing all the cheap, plastic, hideous toys into cheap, plastic, hideous crates ready to be upended at 6 a.m. the next morning. We then try to have a conversation that goes sort of like:

I'm real tired.

Yeah. So tired.

Yeah, I might just . . .

Yeah. I'm just gonna . . .

Go to bed.

Yeah. Bed.

I mean it's almost 9.30 . . .

Shit, is it that late?

The only wooden toys we own are the ones I bought when

I was pregnant with my first. Eddie picked them up once. And then put them back down again.

Yesterday, he played with those awful bloody Countdown dominoes for an hour and a half! And still — many, many months after I put all his Countdown cards on TradeMe in a fit of rage — he asks me for his 'faveybit cards, dear Mama? Wea they gone, my Mama?'

I don't know, son. They're just gone.

I WILL NEVER HAVE MY KIDS IN BED WITH ME. THEYRE MEANT TO BE IN A COT.

wheeze laugh that turns into sobbing

I WILL NEVER LET MY KID INTO THE TOILET WHILE I'M GOING. IT'S WEIRD. I DON'T UNDERSTAND THESE PARENTS WHO LET THEIR KIDS WATCH THEM.

Aged three months: Peeing and holding a screaming baby because the decibel level is slightly lower when you're holding them compared to when they're on the floor. Internal monologue: *I am so tired I think I've forgotten how to pee.*

Aged one year: Little hands under the door. Heavy breathing/screaming/banging on bottom of the door. Internal monologue: *I am so tired it feels so good to sit down!* External monologue: Mama is coming, honey! Hold on! Hold on, my beautiful angel baby sweetheart! Hold on! OK, hol—Wait . . . No tears, I'll be out soon . . . OK, hol—Wait . . .

Aged one-and-a-half: Door suddenly opens to ecstatic toddler looking like a teenager who has just found their parents' booze stash. External monologue: HOW DID YOU OPEN THE DOOR?!

Aged two: Toddler playing at your feet. Occasionally staring into bowl. There is no other monologue but toddler monologue: Why you pee dear Mama? Why? Why you sit down like dat? Why you sit? Wea you bum is? Wea you toilet? You nee paper? Me see? Me see you bum? Mama? Wha choo doin? Wha choo doin now? (It's still a monologue because you're not even able to answer.)

Aged almost three: External monologue: My darling! Mama is going to the toilet! Come and see! Everybody poos on the toilet because pooing on the toilet is so fun! Look! Do you want to poo on the toilet? Digger drivers poo! Elsa poos! Ballet dancers poo! Bob the Builder poos! Daddy poos! Teddy poos! Everybody poos! *slightly hysterical now* EVERYBODY POOS. OK?!

MY KIDS ARE GOING TO LISTEN TO REAL MUSIC.
No, they're not. They're going to listen to 'Let It Go' a thousand times a day and you're going to deal with it.

I like to think most people aren't as moronic as I was pre-kids. I really had lots of ideas that disappeared along with my waist and ability to sleep for seven hours uninterrupted. But the biggest one for me was this one:

I WONT CHANGE
Having children has been the most profound and incredible experience of my life and it has changed every little and big bit of my being. Every bit.

Holding my baby for the first time shattered me into a million pieces, quickly reordered by his first breath into someone willing to lay my life down for him a million times over.

Seeing my husband curled around our babies, rocking them to sleep and humming gently, swelled my heart until the blood rushed into my cheeks — a warm glow I still feel every time he lovingly cuddles them back to slumber.

My son's first surgery ripped me into shredded ribbons that I quickly threaded back together ready to be the whole person he needed when he came back to me.

The first time someone said something hurtful about my child turned my spine to ice, set my bones to concrete, my blood to fire.

When we held our second baby in our arms — who knew it would be that same crushing feeling? That overwhelming, almost painful joy?

The pride that makes me feel bigger and stronger than I am when I see our little boy show kindness and compassion for others. That wonder — how on earth did we get so lucky?

And all the little times we reassess and change or decimate or ignore the silly little ideas we had about what kind of parents we thought we would be — almost every hour, always every day — the values stay the same. We want kind kids who feel safe and loved. But all the little ideas are blown away by an imaginary leaf-blower, powered by a little boy who is almost three and knows a lot more than his mum a lot of the time.

Certainly knows more than his mum did before she became his mum.

HOW TO GET YOUR BABY TO SLEEP

Getting your baby to sleep is really quite simple.

TIRED SIGNS

Some people say look for tired signs, but actually you should look for signs that your baby might be about to do tired signs. Before there are tired signs, make sure you put your baby down to sleep. Immediately.

Try to connect telepathically to your child — ask them: are you tired but not so tired that you're showing tired signs?

Tired-but-not-too-tired signs are varied. They generally sound like cooing, screaming, crying, blowing raspberries, strong language and singing R&B classics from the '90s.

Sometimes there is no sound.

Is baby biting their fist? Opening their mouth? Sticking out their tongue? Do they have a tongue? Are their eyes open? Are they closed? Did they blink? Did they move their body in any way? Did their foot twitch? Did they move their arm?

These are tired signs. This means baby is tired.

You have a window of .36 of a second to get your baby into their cot.

SLEEPING ENVIRONMENT

Do not let them sleep in your bed or room or they will never leave home. They'll be 57 and you'll be on your death bed but you won't be actually in your death bed because they'll be in your bed. You'll be on the floor. Miserable, and not because you're dying. Death will be a sweet release.

Do not let them sleep in the bouncer. They will grow up to be one of those people who doesn't stand up for old ladies on the bus. They'll call you from London on their OE and say they just need to borrow $8000. And they'll always forget your birthday and they won't call till really late on Mother's Day. They'll borrow the car but never put petrol in it. You're going to be buying their clothes when they're 49. Is that what you want? All because you let them sleep in the bouncer.

Do not let them sleep in a mini-crib or Moses basket past 39.7 days old. You will regret it. They will literally, literally, *literally* never sleep again and it will be your fault because you're a terrible mother.

Let them sleep in the buggy if you want them to be held back in Year 3 and never be able to do basic arithmetic.

Get back to nature. Leave them in a tree.

The ideal sleep environment is Nanna's house.

SLEEP ROUTINE

Once they're in the cot, hold your hand above them and kiss their forehead but not with too much affection. Kind of like if someone else's child went to kiss you on the lips but you know they had a vomiting bug a few days before so you kind of dodge them while still letting them kiss you. Kiss your baby like that.

Take a step to the right, put your hands on your hips and pull your knees in tight.

If they wake, pick them up. Then put them down. Then pick them up. Then put them down. Then pick them up. Then put them down. Then pick them up. Then put them down. Then pick them up. Then pick them up. Wait! If you can do that, that means you put them down again! You've got to start over now.

Pick them up, put them down, then pick them up, down, up, put them down now. Pick them up.

Then put them down.

Do this for around 72 hours.

If your baby still isn't sleeping, it's likely they're overstimulated. Remove all furniture including their cot from your house. Put in white carpet. Put white padding on the walls. Doesn't that look better? Now you can sit in the corner and rock in peace.

Place baby in the centre of a pentagram and finish sacrificing your goat to the sleep gods.

Baby is also under-stimulated. You need to get the sweet spot where they're just stimulated. Pop up and down from behind the cot — if this terrifies baby, you're overstimulating them. If they don't scream, you've under-stimulated baby.

Rocking and shushing can help. Rock your baby for around 22 hours. Then shush your baby. Try to shush every six seconds. If you shush every seven seconds you will have to repeat the process over again. Do this for around eight months.

Put them down awake but a bit asleep. Baby should have one eye open and one eye closed and one eye kind of half-open and half-closed so you're not sure if they're awake or asleep.

FEEDING AND WEANING

Feed them to sleep.

Just kidding. Never feed them to sleep. Are you crazy? What is wrong with you?

Shoot breast-milk across the room into their mouth. Make them beg for a bottle. Otherwise they'll grow up soft.

Don't spoil them with food. Food is not a necessity. It's a luxury. A luxury your greedy baby can quite frankly do without.

Think about it — have you ever climbed into bed and then

wanted a glass of water or a snack? Have you ever woken up during the night and wanted a sip of water? Been suddenly hungry? No, that has never, ever happened.

Use logic — is it more likely that your tiny baby is manipulating you and actually hates your guts and wants you to never sleep? Or are they maybe a bit thirsty?

Exactly: they're all manipulating jerk babies that hate you *and* hate sleep.

Give them solids even if they're six hours old. If it was good enough for a cave baby with a life expectancy of 17, it's good enough for your baby.

SLEEP AIDS

Use sleep drops or opium.

Swaddle your baby until they're 22 minutes old. And then until they're 4.92 months old. Swaddle them tightly enough that they feel like they're trapped in a cold and cruel world, but not so tight that their circulation is cut off.

Only use muslin wraps. Clean the wraps with your bitter tears.

Put on some (Barry) White noise.

But remember, if you use white noise they'll never be able to sleep without it ever and you've created a rod for your back and, really, you should have thought about that before you had children. Isn't it a shame that you can't do anything right when that other mum in your coffee group has a baby that actually asks her, in three different languages, to put him down for a sleep?

Your baby may settle when you cuddle them, but this is just your baby being spiteful. When you're not around they call their baby friends and laugh about you behind your back.

Check the temperature of the room. It's probably too hot and too cold.

Get a night light, but never turn it on.

Now that you know how to get your baby to sleep, make sure you tell other mums how to get their babies to sleep. If yours sleeps, theirs should, too. Because all babies are the same. Here are some helpful things you can say to mothers of babies about sleep:

'I slept through the night from birth.'

'My child basically hasn't woken up since I got home from the hospital.'

'That's interesting, my friend's baby was like that and it turned out the baby had Horrible Disease with Awful Prognosis.'

'Babies need sleep or else they won't develop properly.'

'I think babies need tough love.'

'I don't know why people become parents if they're not willing to die or become severely ill from sleep deprivation.'

'It's actually easy to get babies to sleep; other mums just over-think it.'

'My child sleeps *too* much! It's a nightmare.'

If none of these suit you, you could just randomly yell incoherently about 'mums these days'.

Goodnight. See you in 45 minutes.

BIRTH EXPERIENCES

Your body knows what to do in birth.

You'll never have a baby too big to be pushed out.

Nobody really needs a Caesarean.

Drugs in birth will mean your baby is born drugged.

STOP.

We need to stop this stuff. We really do.

It's an absolute calamity — just a horrible, awful, terrible thing — that so many mothers are beginning their lives as mothers with horrible stuff about birth clanging away in their heads.

There is a place for advocacy around birth. I am a supporter of the midwifery system. I think we are incredibly lucky in New Zealand to have this system. And I think it saves lives.

But the birth-advocacy movement has a problem when so many mothers feel they can't talk about their births because the dialogue has been hijacked. Absolute falsehoods about every mother being capable of a vaginal birth if they just *tried harder* are out there, being peddled as truth.

When a mother should just be free to work through her feelings about birth, and recover from her experience (as we all must do in some way or another), she's getting these messages. And what concerns me is they're meant to be from a place of empowerment — but they're just not. They're landing like blows on mothers who are already bruised.

The experiences we have bringing our children into the world are so complex. We have dreams and hopes and desires of what their births will be like. We have society telling us that the safe delivery of a baby is all that matters — a far too simplistic view that takes away the agency of a mother, but a view that is also very true, and is a lifeline to many mothers who are recovering from traumatic births.

We need to allow space for women to tell the stories of their births, and we need to create room for them to decide how they feel about their experiences.

Because some will feel emotional pain as well as the obvious physical pain. And some won't. Some will be unsure, and it will take a while to fully appreciate how they feel.

The feelings of these women, the story of how lives came to be, cannot be co-opted by others. Nobody can tell the story of your baby's birth except you.

So when we try to create a dialogue that isn't ours, we need to stop.

We need to stop before we say 'Are you upset it was a C-section?' or 'Was a forceps delivery really bad?'

This is one of our first chances with a new mother to let her know that she alone decides what value or feeling is placed on her birth experience. That she alone decides what to share and what not to share, and her truth is what matters.

When you can't pick up your child because you've had major abdominal surgery, when you've got a packet of frozen peas in your undies and you're sitting on a pad the size of a surfboard — you don't need a lecture or to be told how you should feel.

We need to begin as we mean to go on.

Support not sanctimony. Truly hearing. Not waiting to speak, or deciding what will be said before she gets to talk.

Advocacy is actually about really listening. There's just not enough of that out there.

FAVOURITE THINGS

reee

Eddie: I need to make my dear mama a present of all her favite tings and dat tings are:

Lots of wines and choc-an-lits and money for them.

And my deddy's favite tings are my mama and beers.
And lollies.

I feel as if the amount of emphasis on our drinking is slightly unfair . . .

THEY LISTENED

~

Breastfeeding Nazis. Nipple Nazis. The Breastapo. Breast-feeding police. Psychos. Smug Earth Mother bitches. Sanctimummies. Bullies. Anti-formula fanatics.

Did you hear the one about that mother whose baby died because she'd been *brainwashed* by lactation consultants? They're mum-bashing do-gooders. They hate formula. They hate women. They should get rid of La Leche League. They're a bunch of dangerous hippies.

That's just a sample of what people say about lactation consultants in your average article about breastfeeding in New Zealand.

Well, here's what I have to say about them: they listened to me. They heard me. When I felt desperately alone, they were there for me. They empowered me. They made me feel strong. They wiped away my tears. They made me feel like I'm a good mother and I should be proud of myself. They made me feel like I mattered, too. That I could trust myself as a mother.

I always thought breastfeeding would be easy. I had always wanted to breastfeed. I tried so very hard with my first-born. But I was too scared to ask for help. I'd been told by absolutely everyone that lactation consultants would yell at me. They're anti-formula, I was told. They're judgemental. I didn't ask for help because I was afraid of them.

While my oldest son was in hospital I tried to advocate for myself, and for him. 'I want to keep breastfeeding', I told the doctors and nurses and registrars and well-meaning family. I kept being told my milk was the problem. In my head I felt that couldn't be right. Why couldn't I just give him expressed breast-milk in a bottle? Why did it have to be formula?

Alone and utterly exhausted and emotionally ruined, I gave him formula in hospital at 3 a.m. I weaned in agony in a children's ward on my own. Every time a child near me cried, my breasts did, too. I was never able to comfort him at the breast again.

I remember sobbing and asking a nurse, 'How do I stop the milk?' She just said, 'We can't give you anything' and walked off. Another said, 'There's nothing wrong with formula, for goodness' sake!'

I'd never, ever suggested that there was anything wrong with formula. I got mastitis in both breasts while trying to look after my desperately ill child.

I'm not anti-formula. I formula-fed my son. I am very grateful for formula. But I will never be thankful for the way I was railroaded into giving up on breastfeeding. It really hurt me. And for a long time I swallowed that hurt, because when I tried to voice it people jumped down my throat: don't you think you've got bigger things to worry about? There's nothing wrong with formula. Your son gained weight. Isn't he the priority? Shouldn't you put your son first? Actually, formula is better than breast-milk because you know what's in formula. Who cares how you feed your baby? Get a grip. You should have really started him on formula earlier. All that matters is that your son is healthy. You're being a bit dramatic, aren't you?

I felt silenced at every turn. I didn't dare express how I felt. I knew how I should feel — I should know that what I wanted wasn't important. That my instincts were wrong. That wanting to breastfeed was selfish if I couldn't do it immediately, without any hassles. Sick children should be given formula. Breast-milk is too unreliable. It was irresponsible, even dangerous, definitely self-absorbed and narcissistic, to want to breastfeed if it was difficult or if my child had health problems. I was anti-formula and judgemental of mothers who used formula if I didn't use it when I was told to. Breastfeeding was just a way to feed your child — it had no other worth. It didn't matter how you fed, just feed — but with formula.

Even now, I find it so hard to trust my own feelings because of the gaslighting and stress of it all.

When my second son was born, I was absolutely determined that I would make the choice as to whether I breastfed or not. I wouldn't let anyone else take that choice from me.

The first people to listen to me were my midwives. One of my midwives was training to be a lactation consultant. In tears, I told her about my weaning the first time. She listened. She never called me dramatic or told me off for the feelings I had. She held my hand.

I left the hospital a few hours after my second was born and she came over to help me with my latch. She then came over again a few days later. She kept texting me and sending me online messages to troubleshoot the problems I was having. She did all of this voluntarily.

Being a midwife is an exhausting job — it means long hours, and emotionally it requires huge resilience. I am astounded that on her days off she still took the time to visit me to help me feed.

I messaged her at 2 a.m. when my youngest son was in hospital and I was again in a vulnerable position, with formula being offered at every possible opportunity. She immediately responded. She sent me love and encouragement and said she would come to the hospital to help me.

What a Nazi!

When my son was two months old I went to the Newtown Breastfeeding Support Clinic. I walked in and immediately started sobbing. The volunteer there gave me a glass of water and a hug — and she listened to me. Another volunteer entertained my toddler while they helped me with the pain I was having in one of my breasts. I felt completely safe in that hall, surrounded by other mums struggling through like I was.

Every single week these women gather and sit in a hall and help mums breastfeed. Voluntarily. They give up those hours with their children to help us with our children.

Bullies, right?

Those lactation consultants kept emailing me to make sure I was OK — physically and emotionally. Not once did they pressure me to breastfeed or bottle-feed. I was given help with the pain and we discussed what the reasons could be for it. They told me they could give me help with weaning if I chose to do that and kept in close contact with me.

Smug, right? Anti-formula fanatics? Totally.

But La Leche League are the worst, aren't they?

In agony one afternoon, I called a number on the La Leche League website. A woman answered. I could hear her children in the background. I was completely hysterical. I could barely get words out. She told me to take deep breaths and calmed me down enough to get details from me.

This volunteer, a stranger, offered to come to me if I needed immediate help. She encouraged me to contact my husband and get him to come home and take me to my GP. This might all sound melodramatic, but if you're surviving on no sleep, and you're in extreme pain, and you're overwhelmed — it's impossible to think straight.

This woman voluntarily takes calls from sobbing mothers, day in and day out, and talks them off ledges.

I ended up in A&E, where a doctor gave me tramadol. I was a mess on it.

I was told by almost everyone to just stop breastfeeding. I

know why. I know it is well meaning. I know I am stubborn. But it was so hard to hear that.

I was never told to stop or keep going by lactation consultants. I was never dismissively told 'Happy mum, happy baby!', as if wanting to breastfeed was a terrible thing to do to my child. I was never told 'You don't have to breastfeed, you know' or 'I don't know why you're bothering' or 'It's not compulsory', as if I was a complete moron who doesn't know her own mind.

I wasn't ever pressured by anyone to breastfeed.

I wanted to.

Desperately.

The only time I was ever given permission to feel this way was when I was around lactation consultants.

This is mainly just about my appreciation for them. I managed to get through my youngest son's hospital stay without stopping breastfeeding. I am proud of myself for that. I trusted my gut and he gained weight on breast-milk. I knew he would. I know my milk is working well for him. But it has taken me a long time to trust myself. And I trust myself because of them.

Now I feed on one side, as the other boob is some weird cosmic mess that is super-painful. But I feed! I did it!

I now breastfeed without pain. My son is pink and fat like a delicious Christmas ham.

I could not have done it without lactation consultants. They protected me. Supported me. Comforted me.

More than anything, they listened to me. And here I am — finally, four months on, feeding my baby easily.

I got to heal myself, and that matters.

I'm not going to buy into the narrative that lactation consultants are monsters. If you need help with breastfeeding, then go to them! Your feelings matter.

I'm so incredibly grateful that so many women block out the

horrific abuse they get in every article about their profession, every thread online, in mum groups, on Twitter, on Facebook, at coffee groups — everywhere — to voluntarily listen every day to women who need help.

GOODNIGHT AND GOOD LUCK

I am really tired.

If you're reading this and you're a parent of young children you're probably very tired, too. I wanted to write this, though, because it's basically all I'm thinking about right now. How tired I am.

Days are quite foggy. Dull throbbing behind my eyes is normal. I'm often caught staring into space, trying to recapture a long-gone train of thought. I try not to snap and to stay perky and cheery. But I am honest with my toddler — *Mama is tired. I'm sorry for getting angry, but I'm just a bit tired and when you're tired everything is a bit hard* . . . I think it's important not to hide from kids the reality of . . . I don't know: this life.

Sundays are hard. The week looms ahead and you don't know how much sleep — if any — is ahead. It feels a bit overwhelming. You want to prepare for the week ahead, have to, but getting off the couch feels like climbing Mt Everest.

It seems a silly thing to write about, but gosh, I never realised how tiring this whole parenting lark would be. How tiring it is. Not sleeping, of course; that *just falling asleep and then the baby cries out*. Or *finally falling heavily into dreams and then you're catapulted out by a toddler touching your face*.

Side note: Is your toddler terrifying at night? The other night mine started singing 'Where is pinky? Where is pinky? Run away! Run away!' — *terrifying*. In my half-dead/half-asleep state I do not need to see a shadow in the hall and hear that tiny sing-song voice floating through the house. There are enough people in this house who regularly shit their pants, thank you very much.

Where was I? Tired. Everyone says: you will be tired. And of course you know this, of course you do. But you can't prepare for it. And three years into this parenting thing I'm still struck dumb by how exhausting it is. I'm used to it now — used to not getting more than three hours' sleep at a time. But that doesn't mean it doesn't sometimes feel like my life is a slow car-crash.

Because as I said, it's not just the waking up to babies and toddlers and all of that. And also the getting so used to not sleeping you can't sleep even when they don't wake up. It's the emotional and physical and everyday exhaustion, too: needing to be patient, considered, answering 80 trillion questions a day, picking up clothes, changing nappies, not having time to yourself. That stuff is just depleting. It's just *hard*.

And I often think the following three things:

1. THERE ARE OTHER PARENTS NOT SLEEPING. RIGHT? WHAT IF THEY ARE SLEEPING? NOBODY ELSE SEEMS THAT TIRED.

I am sure not sleeping is the norm, but we just whack on a smile because what are you going to do about it? No point moping, right? Complaining won't change anything. I do believe that; if I go on and on about how tired I am I feel even more tired.

But sometimes it's so good to hear another mum talking about how her kids aren't sleeping. It really is. And not in a 'yay, you're exhausted, too' way. Just a 'that's right, this is normal' way. Because otherwise it's so easy to think everybody else's kids are sleeping but yours aren't.

When it's 3 a.m. and I've been up every few hours, thinking there are other mums doing this, too, makes me feel better. It just does. Knowing that we all struggle sometimes. And we are all tired. It makes me feel normal.

And it's normal to not get sleep. Not to get on my high horse, but 'society' wants us to believe that it's not normal for kids to be up during the night. Baby sleep-training experts are all about this narrative that your kid is messed up because they don't sleep 12 hours from birth. They're wrong. It's normal.

2. IS IT MY FAULT THAT MY KIDS DONT SLEEP?

Again, my rational brain tells me that it's not my fault my kids aren't sleeping. They're sick, their routines have been out of whack, it's normal developmental stuff. But we live in a world where we are told that babies sleep through from eight weeks old. And if I so much as yawn in public someone tells me how to get my kids to sleep through the night.

And the thing is — I'm fine with what I'm doing. You may think I shouldn't have my kids coming into bed with me, or I should not breastfeed them to sleep, or use a swaddle, or not use a swaddle, not use white noise, not allow them to have a bottle or a night feed or a night light or whatever. But it means nothing to you. I have tried everything under the sun and you know what works? Everything and nothing.

When kids sleep through, they sleep through, and there is no magic formula. There is no threshold they cross where they sleep through from then on. Some months they might sleep well. Some weeks they might not. Children are like adults — some are good sleepers, some are not. Some need a lot of help to get to sleep and stay asleep, some don't.

I went through a period when I was about 20 where I didn't sleep for more than a few hours without waking. It lasted almost a year. Why should a child be any different?

Does this mean I don't blame myself for my kids waking multiple times in a night? Of course not. Because I'm a bit of a dick that way.

3. I'M NEVER GOING TO SLEEP AGAIN.

I know I will. I know this is temporary. But also sometimes I almost have a panic attack at the sheer force of how much my kids need me right now. Right now — I just want to sleep. I want to sleep so bad it hurts. Not a nap here and there but a *real proper five hours*. And that will come, and soon. Eddie had a period of about four or five months where he slept all through the night, and often he does sleep through now — so I know it will happen. I have experience to fall back on. But in the midst of it, sometimes it's hard to keep those illogical thoughts at bay.

This isn't forever. This isn't forever.

And I am tired of feeling lonely in this. I don't often talk about how tired I am, because when I say I'm tired I don't want anyone to tell me what to do about it. I know what to do. I know what suits my parenting style. What feels right for me and my family. I'm not being a martyr because I don't parent the way you — unsolicited advice-giver — do. I don't need advice on how to get them to sleep. I don't need to hear that your kids were sleeping through by the time they were the age my kids are. I'm happy for you — but our kids are different.

You telling me that is as logical as me saying that I sleep all night when you tell me that you have insomnia.

So I guess what I'm saying is — I'm tired.

And to you, if your head is just static white noise and you feel like you might just fall over, I want to say:

You're not alone. I'm tired, too.

It's not your fault your kids aren't sleeping or you can't sleep.

It'll pass.

But right now it's shit.

And I'm sorry about that.

Good luck.

TOP FIVE ASSUMPTIONS

The top five assumptions I had about second children that were intensely wrong — like the most wrong thing that ever was wrong:

1. MY SECOND PREGNANCY WILL BE EASIER THAN THE FIRST.

I puked even more. How is that possible? I was *so sick* the first time. The second time destroyed me. One morning I looked in the mirror and I literally thought 'I think *The Walking Dead* is back on TV soon', based on my appearance. Once someone made a comment about how sick I was and then said they'd heard it was harder for parents who were in their forties when they had their first child. *I was 28!* I don't know why I thought it would be easier. There was no reason at all why it should have been — I'd just decided that it would be. It wasn't.

2. I AM USED TO NOT SLEEPING, SO IT WON'T MATTER IF I DON'T SLEEP FOR A BIT LONGER . . .

A bit longer? *A bit longer? How about no sleep for a year-and-a-half and counting?* What was I thinking? Nobody gets *used* to not sleeping! You keep sort of being alive, but it doesn't get easier! It gets harder! Instead of going two years without sleeping you're now on three years. And you might be used to just a few wake-ups a night, but you're not dealing with 20-plus wake-ups. *For the longest time.* Which leads me to . . .

3. MY FIRST CHILD IS SLEEPING THROUGH NOW SO I'LL ONLY BE WAKING UP TO MY SECOND . . .

Yeah, sure, OK . . . *laughs hysterically* My first-born was waking up fairly regularly when we started talking about having another child. We decided that it would take a long time for me to get pregnant, so he would be five when we would probably be pregnant again. *He was not even two* when we got pregnant. And he slept most nights in bed with me when I was pregnant, yet I still believed that when the baby came he would miraculously sleep through the night in his own bed. *I am not a smart person.* The worst thing ever was having a baby who I had to feed every three hours through the night and a toddler who woke up in between that. *In between*, dear reader. IN BETWEEN THE BITS WHERE YOU WOULD USUALLY HAVE A TINY BIT OF SLEEP THERE WAS NO SLEEP.

4. I WILL KNOW WHAT I'M DOING. SO IT WILL BE EASIER.

I was getting good at parenting my first-born. I was in a good rhythm. My second baby is a totally different baby, who does everything differently, and I have no idea what I am doing all over again. I mean, there are definitely things I didn't do this time around — no baby sensory (sorry kid, but it's expensive and I could just wave my keys in your face and buy a bottle of wine instead, which I need because I have two kids), no tummy time (I don't really want you to be mobile), no pumping (I was *done* after having a more intimate relationship with my pump than I did with my husband — I literally saw that horrible pump more than I saw anyone else), less worrying about things like whether you're getting enough food or sleep. The first time around I kept a ridiculous schedule that noted every feed and for how long, every poo (I didn't weigh them but I, umm, got close to that brand of crazy), every sleep. This time around I am too busy. I feed the baby when he is hungry, try to get him to sleep when he is sleepy. If he doesn't poop for a few days — to be honest, I don't notice. This has made everything way more chill, and reader — I recommend it. *But* . . . I still can't figure out how to get him to sleep (at night or during the day). I worry about his crying — does he cry too much? And I don't know if he is meeting his milestones . . . It isn't easier. It is different. And in some ways it is *harder* — because you have *two babies*. This is simple math. Two = harder than one because there is one more. MATH.

5. I DON'T KNOW IF I WILL HAVE ENOUGH LOVE FOR TWO BABIES.

My big fear when I was pregnant was that I wouldn't have enough love. When I would lean against my big boy's bunk, my hips throbbing and my boobs sore and my baby kicking me to remind me he was coming soon, I would close my eyes and think — what have I got left to give? I would look at my little boy and stroke his golden hair and think, you're too perfect, there's no way another baby could compete with you. And then I held my second son in my arms and my heart just exploded. *You have enough love.* Your heart gets bigger and bigger and you love so much, so much. You have these reserves — more love, more energy, more everything. They're there, and without even realising it you draw on them. And you love your babies even more. Having another baby doesn't divide your love, it multiplies it. You have even more to give because you have to give more. And you love even more than you ever did. Because that's what you need to get through the hard days and nights ahead. More love, more love, more love.

BUILDING A ROUTINE FOR YOUR CHILD

ℓℓℓℓ

Here's a simple routine for getting your child to sleep through the night.

RUN A BATH

Baths are very calming for children. They definitely don't splash and throw toys and crap everywhere, turning your entire bathroom into a chaotic wet mess reminiscent of that awful Kevin Costner film from the '90s. Put in a couple of drops of some overpriced 'sleepy time' bubble bath. It doesn't work of course, but that's not going to stop you from buying more of that shit at 2 a.m. when you're online shopping. What else are you going to do at 2 a.m.?

PUT SOME PYJAMAS ON YOUR BABY

Change a clean onesie into another clean onesie that is deemed a 'bedtime' onesie, because who doesn't love doing 800 loads of washing a day?

PLAY A QUIET GAME

I recommend playing Corpse. That's when you lie on the floor with your eyes closed and allow your child to crawl all over you. It's great imaginative play for your child and it helps them realise the futility of life. Life and death cannot be avoided. Life may feel unending but it will end.

READ TO YOUR BABY

Pick something that suits the mood. How about some Baby Edgar Allen Poe? 'Once upon a midnight dreary, while I pondered, weak and weary . . .'

SING A LULLABY

Anything goes, but probably not 'Big Balls' by AC/DC unless it's going to be an acapella version.

GIVE YOUR BABY A LITTLE MASSAGE

Why not? You're not going to have any time to yourself for *hours*, so you may as well massage your baby. What else are you going to do? Go on Facebook and hate-read all of the irritating status updates from that smug mum in your coffee group who keeps saying her three-week-old baby can say 'I appreciate your efforts at bedtime, Mama' in English, Spanish and Mandarin? You're just going to get angry, so give your baby a massage instead.

KISS YOUR BABY GOODNIGHT

Say 'see you soon' and mean it. Because now begins the four to six hours of shushing and rocking and crying (yours and theirs) before you both eventually pass out from sheer exhaustion.

But at least you spent two hours making sure your child was comfortable and relaxed and ready to scream relentlessly, because you're torturing them by wanting them to sleep at night.

Cherish every moment!

LOVE AND NAPPIES

As I listened through the monitor to my husband trying to get our baby to sleep, I suddenly had a thought that I was pretty sure it was our anniversary. And I'd forgotten to buy him something. As the baby cried, and I listened to my husband quietly singing a song to him, shushing him, gently imploring him to sleep, I thought about our children and how they're clearly the greatest thing to come out of our partnership.

But something else has emerged as well — my husband as a father.

We have been together happily since we met as teenagers. But seeing him as a father makes me feel like I have had the wonderful good fortune of falling in love with a wonderful man twice.

He is an excellent father. We never know when we choose our partners just what kind of parents they will be. We can guess by how they talk about children, how they act around nieces or nephews, slightly tipsy conversations at 3 a.m. . . . but we don't know until we're there, and then there's no going back. I imagine it is the most devastating thing to embark on this journey and find your partner will not step up to be the parent they need to be.

My husband is a different father than I thought he would be. He is as relaxed as I thought he would be — but he also has a determination to be a good father that I didn't expect. He thinks carefully about what kind of parent he wants to be, and he adapts. I knew he would likely roll with the punches, as he always does, but he seems to enjoy the relentlessness of parenting in a way that always surprises me.

Today a journalist came to our house to interview me and some other mothers about antenatal depression. She also talked to my husband. He asked that his face not be shown, as he is notoriously shy — quite the opposite of his mouthy, loud, extroverted wife.

One of the first questions she asked was about sleepless nights. He said he didn't mind as it was 'all part of the job'.

That probably isn't an answer that would delight a journalist — but to me, it says everything about my husband.

And it also says a lot, I think, about love and parenting. Really being there matters. Accepting our children as well as loving them matters. And sometimes love is as simple and as profound as giving up sleep and not minding.

That may not sound very romantic. But actually I believe that great love isn't candles and red roses and extravagant gestures. (I'm generally suspicious of these things . . .)

Great love is putting the baby to sleep again and again and again and again even though it's easier when your partner does it because they have boobs or they smell a certain way or whatever. Great love is gently taking the baby from your partner's arms when they fall asleep feeding them, even though you could just carry on watching TV. Great love is taking over when your partner can't take it anymore. Great love is doing that before it gets to that point. Great love is all of the little things.

You may say well, isn't that just being a parent? And yeah, it is. But many parents don't step up. And it *is* different when you have very, very small children — the burden is usually on the person who spends the most time with the baby. Baby gets used to being close to them, having them put them to sleep, being fed by them . . . all of that relentless day-to-day stuff. As a partner, it would be easy to just say, 'Well, you can get them to bed easier, so you do it' or 'You know how to do a nappy better than I do.'

But this isn't great parenting, and it isn't great love. Because a nappy isn't just a nappy. When you're exhausted, one more nappy can feel like a lot. Like everything.

So on our anniversary I would say to my husband: thank you for all of the nappies. For always being a present husband and father. For never taking the easy option. Thank you for all of the little things.

I would tell him I miss him. Those nights when we don't end up in the same bed because he's in with our toddler and I'm in with our baby — those nights are hard. Or when we're so tired we can't talk. It feels like a long time since we have seen each other, even though we see each other every day and night.

I'd tell him I miss him, but this is worth it and there's nobody else I'd want to be tired with. Nobody else I'd want to share this with. That I think about the years we spent together, just us, and sometimes I feel jealous of the children in his lap — but how I also love that this life suits us so much. Suits him so much.

I'd want him to know that being a great husband and a great dad isn't easy — but it's important. And I love how committed and dedicated he is to being both.

I'd say that seeing him as a dad has made me fall in love with him all over again. That it has been a privilege and I've learned so much from him about how to be a parent. That he's just as important to our little family as I am (even when the baby only wants me — it's just my boobs, I promise).

I'd recite the reading from Louis de Bernières' *Captain Corelli's Mandolin*, which was read at our wedding:

Love is a temporary madness, it erupts like volcanoes and then subsides. And when it subsides you have to make a decision. You

have to work out whether your roots have so entwined together that it is inconceivable that you should ever part. Because this is what love is. Love is not breathlessness, it is not excitement, it is not the promulgation of promises of eternal passion . . .
That is just being 'in love', which any fool can do. Love itself is what is left over when being in love has burned away, and this is both an art and a fortunate accident.

Never has this felt more true than since we became parents.

Love is nappies. And 40 minutes of rocking and shushing and rocking and shushing your crying baby.

Relentless and tiring and tough and strong and beautiful.

A BLESSING

For the mothers carrying babies — I have many hopes for you. Many wishes.

I wish that when your journey toward meeting your beautiful baby begins you're excited as well as scared, because of course it's normal and right to be a little scared. It's a powerful thing we get to do. Isn't it amazing?

I hope you have support and love surrounding you from that first 'is this labour?' thought to that sharp intake of breath when you really know This Is It, and on to your midwife or surgeon telling you it's time. I wish for you that you feel safe from beginning to beginning.

I hope your labour makes you feel powerful or it is just forgettable. That in a week you will gaze at your baby and think 'I could probably do this again'. Look at that beautiful baby you brought into the world. You did it!

When you feed your little one: I wish for every duct to remain unblocked, that you never have to send your partner down the road for cabbage, that your pump is always working. I pray that not a drop of your expressed milk is ever spilled. Not one crack in not one nipple! That's what I hope for you. I hope your supply is just perfect — not too little, not too much. I hope bottles are guzzled with gusto, that formula is on special every time you go to buy it, that your snuggles are extra snuggly as your baby looks up at you, their beloved mama.

I hope you don't accidentally kill someone on Day Three. I wish your hormones to be completely under control. And if they're not, I hope it all goes wrong in a hilariously harmless way that you can tell your coffee group about. I hope it's such a funny story that they laugh with tears in their eyes and tell you that you should be a comedian. And in that moment I hope you feel overwhelmed — not by out-of-control oestrogen, but by the love from your fellow mamas. I wish you to always have a shoulder to cry on, someone to laugh with, someone to make you tea, and someone to gaze at your baby and say as their eyes fill with tears, 'You did so good!'

I hope you never have to clean your house. For at least nine weeks.

I wish that every cry can be easily hushed with a gentle pat. That there are long sleeps and good feeds. That car rides are easy, public transport comes on time, visitors never overstay their welcome. I wish for you chocolate and cider, sleeping on your tummy, comfortable pants and good TV. I hope for visits from friends who have trays of lasagne. I hope for moments where you say, 'It's easier than I thought it would be.'

May you have unobtrusive but excited grandparents. Helpful family. Thoughtful and kind visits. May your buggy brakes never jam, your carrier always work the first time. May there be no poo explosions in white clothes, and no vomit on your good clothes.

Some things I don't have to wish or hope for — I know you will burn with love for your baby. I know those who love you will look at you with eyes shining because they're so proud of you and so in awe of your strength. And I know you're nervous about your first baby and how they'll cope, but I know they'll fall more and more in love with their little brother or sister every single day. Just like you will (because I promise the second time around is just as earth-shattering).

And I also know if none of these things happen, if these wishes don't come true, if these hopes aren't fulfilled, there will be people who you love who are there for you. And you'll do so well anyway — I just know it.

BABY NEEDS MAMA

Lurching into the baby's room as his crying became more and more and more persistent, I found him reaching out to me — his arms and even his fat little fingers calling for me. He was standing on tip-toes in his cot, his body trying to propel himself over the top of the bars. If he fell, he seemed to have utter faith I would catch him.

I lifted him from the cot and he clung to me. Heaving sobs turned to shudders and he pressed his ear firmly to my heart. His breathing slowed and a gentle snoring took over. His fingers relaxed their grip on my arm and I felt his full weight.

He knows what he needs, and what he needs is his mama.

It is all at once an indescribably heavy burden while at the same time making me feel lighter than I ever have before. I am everything to him and he's everything to me. I feel I have so much purpose while being utterly overwhelmed with the strength of that purpose.

Motherhood seems most keenly felt in the wee small hours. Maybe that's why we always describe the night in tiny adjectives. It's so strange to live your early life thinking the night belongs to you. I'm sure it's only in your years before children that you call the night vast and wide. When you have children you realise who the real owners of the night are.

And it's so difficult for others to understand. That you willingly gave your nights away. And you'd give them away again, and again, and again. For the full weight of a baby falling asleep again on your chest. Or a little voice saying 'I had a bad dream, Mama.'

TO MY BABY: I'M SORRY

eeee

My dear sweet baby,

I'm so terribly sorry. It has come to my attention, over the course of writing about raising you, that I have failed you. You see, I have had emails and blog comments and comments on Facebook and tweets, and they have all shown me the error of my ways.

There is so much I must apologise for.

I am sorry for swaddling you. I now know that swaddling restricts not just your limbs as you sleep, but also your creativity and ability to drive a manual car. I am desperately sorry.

I am sorry that studies now show that you are 82 times more likely to be attacked by a swarm of angry bees at the age of 28 because I gave you too much tummy time.

I am sorry that I also didn't give you enough tummy time and you're going to grow up to be a Phil Collins fan who is totally incapable of walking. It has been pointed out to me by an 'expert' that you should be walking by now. And you're not. This must be my fault because you had tap water with fluoride in it. Or it's the tummy time. Or maybe the Bumbo.

That evil Bumbo!

I'm sorry that I gave you a dummy, as a recent study has found that children who were given dummies have a 97 per cent chance of turning into that person at a party who tells you a really, really, really super-long story that goes nowhere and then at the end says, 'I guess you had to be there.'

I'm sorry that I used white noise to get you to sleep. 'Jim' sent me an email 'just because I think you should know'. It turns out the team at FakeScienceToday have found that children who sleep with white noise develop an auditory dependency that inhibits their ability to ride a bike without training wheels. I just wanted you to sleep. But Captain Von Clickbait says that mums who use any kind of sleep aid are basically destroying their children and should be charged with neglect.

I'm sorry I didn't leave you to cry for hours on end, even though the sleep-training consultants say that's what you should do. I wasn't respecting your need to cry yourself to sleep. And now look at you, you haven't slept in 12 years and you have a beard down to your waist and you drink decaf soy chai lattes.

Beards aren't even in fashion anymore.

I am sorry I used Pamol. Those mums in the Real Natural Mums Facebook group were so right: Pamol is a gateway drug to crack cocaine. But at least we have a hobby together now, right?

I am sorry for letting you dress yourself: I have emasculated you, according to a father of seven from Lubbock (I Googled that place and it's in the States). Now you're never going to have a wife, which is apparently very important because how else will you eat if your wife doesn't cook for you, according to this father-of-seven in Lubbock.

I'm sorry I put you in a Jolly Jumper twice in order to take cute/semi-humiliating photos of you. I have been sent a blog post by an anti-Jolly Jumper lobby advocate and she says you're going to grow up to be a 'social media guru'.

I've failed you.

I'm sorry I didn't cut out sugar from your diet. I should have actually read the 8000-word essay I was sent by a parent in Invercargill schooling me on the dangers of sugar. Look at you now, you're that person who talks about sugar for hours at a time. You're incapable of reading social cues.

Oh, I am sorry!

I'm sorry for using a baby carrier. It's true, your legs are useless now — we had to get them removed, and it's so hard to carry you now that you're 47 and weigh 120 kilos. But I brought this on myself, so I will accept it.

I'm sorry I used the buggy instead of the baby carrier — putting you in a front-facing pram is clearly the reason why you live with 15 cats and keep getting told off by the council for hoarding.

I'm sorry I breastfed you and formula-fed you. It's a terrible burden for you to now be both breast-obsessed with 'mommy issues' *and* bottle-obsessed with 'mommy issues'. We have no bond while having too much of a bond. You've been poisoned by Big Formula while also being brainwashed by lactivists. It's all my fault.

What can I say? I tried to do my best, but I should have spent less time parenting and more time reading studies.

I should have stopped listening to you and started listening to what others said about how I should raise you.

I should have read more books instead of just reading you.

I should have kept up with the Joneses (I would never have guessed that university exams would eventually just be one question: What brand of baby muslin did your mother wrap you in on the way home from the hospital?).

I shouldn't have thought that just because I know you best I would know what is best for you.

After all, the people who have actually convinced parents they're messing up their kids' lives by loving them too much — they're the ones we should listen to, right?

Instincts be damned. I should have definitely trusted an email from a stranger over what I know is true in my heart.

Oh well, it's too late for shoulds. I guess we will just have to make sure we tell every mum we meet that they'll be sorry one day, too . . .

Love,

your very sorry Mama

YOU'D NEVER KNOW

When I meet new people, I often have to explain that my son is recovering from a serious respiratory condition. I briefly cover off the fact that he's had a bunch of surgeries and has improved a great deal. I explain that I still need people to be careful around him when it comes to things like colds and flu and getting vaccinated to protect him.

The most common response I get is surprise that he has been through so much and is such a happy child. I am often told 'You'd never know!' and I agree. There's nothing about my rambunctious toddler that screams illness.

You used to be able to hear every breath he took — awake or asleep. We had comments and stares wherever we went. I bloody hated elevators. After each surgery he would be temporarily better. And then the rasping, the dragging breathing, would return.

While writing this I thought I'd look up to see when his last surgery was. It has been a year and I can't believe it. I told someone the other day that it has been six months. I genuinely feel like it was yesterday.

And I can really see how people would think he'd never been so sick — he is the most resilient, strong, brave child. A complete stereotype. The Brave Sick Kid who takes everything thrown at them with a smile.

I wonder, though, how long I will know. Will I ever forget what we have been through as a family?

I'm often asked 'When will you write about Eddie's illness?' I can understand that statement, too. My first year and a half of being a parent was completely dominated by his illness. It is the elephant in the waiting room.

I've tried. I've tried to write about it. To tell his story in a start to (almost) finish kind of way. But I can't. My brain seems to open doors only to little snapshots of memories. But then the door slams shut. I am wired for self-care now. I cannot put that pain into any kind of order. I push myself out before I get in too deep.

Little snapshots.

Eddie at three months old in intensive care after surgery. I don't know what time it is — I have turned off my phone to try to avoid calls in which there is too much silence on the other end. I can't meet the demands for updates. I'm out at sea. My husband is my lighthouse. Nobody can reach us. They are trying to get my baby to breathe on his own, and when they tried to remove the tubes something happened and alarms went off and I was pushed out of the way.

I thought about what would happen if I lost my baby. I thought about the buses that hurtle down the road outside the hospital. Doing it right outside the hospital wouldn't be ideal, though. And it would not be fair on the bus driver.

On the phone to my sister. We had gone in to hospital because Eddie's breathing sounded particularly bad. They are rushing him in for surgery, I tell her. Can she tell the rest of the family that he's going in? I wonder why my arm hurts. I look at it and I have gripped it so tightly that it is now a deep, dark purple.

Is it months later? Or weeks? My husband and I are holding our little boy still. They are guiding a camera into his throat. He has had this procedure so many times. He is bucking and screaming. He goes limp. His skin is pale and clammy. Tears are streaming down my face. 'It's harder on the parents than the child,' someone says. I know that isn't true.

I yawn at work. I have spent the night in hospital again. It is so noisy there that I can't sleep. Eddie doesn't sleep either. Someone says that the trick to getting your child to sleep through the night is to put them in another room with the door shut.

Sitting in the toilet at work, sobbing. He needs more surgery. I can't work out why I'm not getting better at handling this. I have a meeting in eight minutes. Why does it feel like it's getting harder? I feel like I can't breathe and I wonder if this is how he feels every day and that thought alone makes my jaw ache and my heart beat faster until I feel dizzy and cold.

I am exhausted. A woman in a café asks what's 'wrong' with my son. I say he has a respiratory condition. My body language is clearly telling her that I do not want to talk about it. 'Should you have him out in this weather?' she asks. I say through gritted teeth that he's fine. 'Have you tried amber beads? My daughter swears by them for her son and he has asthma, too.' I imagine pouring boiling water over her and the thought makes me smile. Another mother frowns at the rasping noises coming from the buggy. She raises an eyebrow at her friend. My smile disappears.

A friend brings over their child. They have a snotty nose. It's just allergies, she says. I spend the next week sleeping no more than two or three hours a night. I am convinced he will get sick and end up in hospital again.

We are hopeful. We are daring to think he might be better after nearly three months of silent breathing. Then in the morning we hear him gasping. Overnight his breathing returns to the familiar dragging. We know that this means more surgery.

In a Facebook group a woman rants about how Pamol is poison. She treats her son's teething pain with cuddles, she says. He's never been vaccinated and that's why he doesn't get sick. Whooping cough is just a cough, she says. No children have died of whooping cough, and if they did it's a form of natural selection. I lie awake at night thinking about how I can keep him safe. I can feel his breath on my chest as he snuggles into me. I kiss his forehead and know I will do anything to protect him, but how can I protect him from people like that?

I am grateful that my husband handles all of Eddie's medications. There is only one where he needs to be held down so we can give it to him. The rest he has gotten used to taking.

I am pregnant. 'Are you worried the baby will be like Eddie?' somebody asks.

All of these little snapshots don't begin to tell the story. He is getting better. He is better. Is he better?

Sometimes I feel like every little bit of this particular pain has attached to my bones. It is a weight that I carry around always, and I wonder when it will be lifted. When will enough time have passed for it to pass? I feel like all of the time we fought for him to breathe, it was a war. We have returned from the front shell-shocked. What is the length of time you need to be home for it to go away?

I think parents who go through this have some kind of sick kid post-traumatic stress disorder. The people around you get sick-kid fatigue. They have enough sympathy for the first few surgeries, but your child is meant to just get better or . . . well . . . Limbo is a strange thing.

And when they do get better, you're supposed to be free from it all, too. Your child is better! That's it. That's the end of that story. Please begin talking about the lessons you've learned. Preferably have some Hallmark-card quotes ready. Everyone loves a happy ending.

But it isn't over, even when it's meant to be over. The fear is always there. Particularly when it's a chronic illness or a condition that isn't well understood. Remission or recovery doesn't erase the past.

Last week he built an adventure in our lounge. You had to

leap from the couch onto the pillows. Jump them like a monkey. Climb onto the recliner and leap onto the carpet, which is the sea. Watch out for the shark! You're a pirate now. Walk the plank then begin again. He does this 10 times.

I hear a ragged edge to his breathing.

I feel that familiar ache in my shoulders. The dull pain in my neck. The heat on my face. My eyes prickle.

My heart jumps.

Will I always know?

LOVELY WORDS

I'm in hospital with my son. We have been here all week. I have been too tired to write anything coherent. My brain is a jumble of words. I have written bits and pieces over the last few days. Here are some feelings. Some things I've been thinking. Not particularly eloquent, but I wanted to put them out there anyway.

There are some lovely words.

Ya'aburnee is a word commonly used in Lebanon. It is Arabic, and it is difficult to translate. It is the wish that you will die before the one you love. Simply: you bury me.

Unsurprisingly, it is a sentiment that lives mostly in the hearts of mothers. I have watched my two babies fragile in their hospital beds, fighting for breath, too many times now. Each time *ya'aburnee* escapes from my lips as a whisper, a fervent prayer.

It is the same every time — when my babies are at rest, their chests still straining but their eyes closed, I too close my eyes. I picture them at peace and content with loved ones, partners, children, grandchildren, friends, cuddles, kisses, travel, wine, cheese, trampolines, laughter, happy tears, celebrations. I picture them proudly watching recitals, performances, gigs, shows, races — karate, swimming, guitar, ballet? I picture them at graduations, awards, writing CVs, creating art. I picture them with a faceless love by their side who brings them as much joy as their father brings me. And I imagine them saying 'Your Nanna used to say . . .' to their grown children in remembrance of me. And even though I'm gone, they're not broken by my absence. They have their own beautiful lives now. And they look at their babies and whisper *ya'aburnee*.

❂

If a woman's work is never done, a mother is never allowed to rest. I am told to rest. To sleep. To 'have a cup of tea'. I hate tea. It tastes like dirt. I am fuelled by coffee.

I am anchored to my son's cot. I am a lumbering ship. Slow. Not in the best condition, really. But determined. I need things to be repeated. I don't understand what the doctors say to me the first time around. I cry in private. It is too hard to rest. When I sleep, it is through sheer force. My body drags me down into the ground and it's dark and cool . . . and then a cry launches me up. My body acts before my brain does. *I am here, it's OK, I am here. I will rest later.*

My second boy came into the world screaming. His face was a deep purple. He was big and he was born angry, screaming at the sky. I love that fight in him.

His labour was long, far too long. He fought to be here, to be heard, and he fights to stay here. He seems so resilient even as he struggles.

I did not have drugs during his labour because I did not want to be away from my Eddie overnight. It was agony. I felt like my pain could crack the sky. But it wasn't as painful as being away from my Eddie for so many days now. My arms feel empty. I long to kiss his forehead. To push his dirty blond hair from his face. To hear his incessant chatter.

The ward, even with the crying, the constant alarms, the yelling, the sound of so much marching past our door, sounds too quiet without his relentless commentary. I saw him briefly and he said to me 'You OK my darling? My dear Mama?' He is so compassionate. He is a born mother. A study in care and empathy.

Missing someone even when you know they're close and not gone can feel like physical pain. I just know I never want to be apart from my babies.

●

This place is misery. Surely, there is no sadder, more isolated place than the children's ward in a hospital.

Mothers rock even when their babies aren't in their arms. Fathers have red-rimmed eyes. Their shoulders are tense. Their footsteps are the heaviest.

Nurses are patient, but parents are quick to anger. There is so much crying, screeching, babies in pain — but I think the worst cry is the lonely, desperate crying in the night of parents who just want their babies to get better. Torture is not being able to fix your baby. To not be able to hold them because of tubes and monitors and cords like delicate ropes that feel like they're strangling you. To stand with teeth clenched, nails digging into your arms, as strangers work, speaking a language you don't understand, too busy to translate, on your precious baby — it is a specific type of hell.

But there is so much humanity here, too. The doctor who gently sings a lullaby to your baby as he tries to get a line in. The nurse who gets you a hot chocolate just because you look like you need one. The texts and tweets and calls and financial support because heaven knows nothing is more terrifying than not being able to pay your bills when you're in here. The man at the coffee stand who remembers your order and starts making it so you don't have to speak through tears. The other parents who nod and say 'Need anything?' No energy for themselves, but they are machines with one setting — to care for their babies, and anyone else who needs it right now. Because we share this hell together.

●

I will get to leave. My baby will be OK. But some won't. And I weep for them. Nobody should ever have to bury their child.

Every time I leave hospital I have a renewed dedication to frantic, compulsory empathy and compassion for others. The world is too mean, too often. We have to be kinder. Always. Gentle. Always. Because some people never get to leave here.

WHEN TIME STANDS STILL

As I rocked (quite vigorously, I must say) my baby to sleep and attempted again to get the dummy into his mouth, I thought to myself 'Ughh, I can't wait till he is older and we are through with this bloody stage.' I thought the same as he yet again pulled his brother's wooden toy kitchen onto his head, screaming and wailing as a big egg formed above his eye.

Ughh, can't we just skip the pulling-things-over phase and go straight to the can-balance-without-destroying-self stage?

Can't I be done with breastfeeding? I want him to be able to take a bottle so I can go out or, better still, drink water out of a cup so I don't have to keep washing bottles.

I do it less with my older son but it's not unusual for me to think 'I can't wait until he's old enough for sleepovers.' Or 'It'll be good when he's big enough for the top bunk so we can move Ham in and they can share a room.'

I often find myself thinking 'I really want them to be at the play-independently-and-read-a-book stage. Just long enough for me to fill the dishwasher and drink a coffee that's actually hot.'

And then my Eddie will say, 'I want a hold?' and I will scoop him up and be shocked by the weight, how his legs now skim past my knees. How can those little arms fit right around my neck when fat little fingers could barely meet before?

And then he fiercely says, 'No I do myself!' and puts up a warning arm at me. I watch as he pulls on his gumboots, a huge smile forming as he relishes his independence.

I remember his first shoes, soft and green with a little

dinosaur on them. How he was so tiny when he first started walking that he used to rest his head behind my knees. Those little shoes scuffing along as he took tiny steps, arms reaching out for me. How he used to put one arm around each leg.

I remember how I struggled to put on those gumboots only a few months ago and thought 'Ughh, I can't wait until he can do this himself.'

I remember when he was born and could fit in a shoebox. And now he stretches out on his bunk bed, a million soft toys around him. But Icy — the one he loved the most when he was tiny, with a chewed ear that saw all of his teeth come through — is discarded now. Replaced by Teddy Bear and Sally and Other Sally (I have no idea).

And I look at my enormous baby tearing across the room on all fours, and I can't remember when he first started crawling because I feel like we only just welcomed him into the world, yet he will be one *this month*. And he's going to walk any minute now and how is it possible that a baby that was just born one minute ago is walking?

Yet his first 11 months were the longest 11 months that ever existed.

And I want time to stand still just as I want it to rush on. And it does stand still — hours and hours are so long and exhausting and you're rocking and shushing or negotiating or calming or cajoling and it takes days but you see that it's minutes.

How is it possible that minutes feel like days but a year is gone in a minute?

I don't want my babies back, but I want them to stay my babies forever. I am so immensely proud when I see my son do something he's been trying to do for ages — taking off the pen lid, or writing an 'E', or remembering what comes after eight. But I also fight the urge to say 'Stop! You're my little baby! Stay with me, baby.'

And I want my baby to walk as much as he wants to walk, but I know I won't be able to pinpoint the moment those fat little legs stop being so wide and unsure with their steps and became sturdy and strong.

This is the nature of these lives that we're privileged to watch unfold in front of us. In a heartbeat the moments are gone, but it doesn't matter so much when your heart is full.

You can't trap a moment and keep it with you. Our babies are too busy to give us time to get misty-eyed.

NATURAL PARENTING

My baby sleeps through the night. It's really easy to get them to sleep through. I mean, mine was sleeping through from probably about six and a half minutes post-birth. But I think that's in part due to the way we gave birth to her — I say 'we' because my heart partner and yoga guru Trent simulated birth alongside me so that we could both experience the joyous wonder and orgasmic power of labour together. It was important we begin our co-parenting journey together in that way, you know? Vaginally.

Well yes, the midwife didn't like it. She said she felt uncomfortable that Trent was naked and covered in home-made vernix — but we stood our ground and got the birth we wanted. I think midwives need to accept that times are changing, and I'm sure that there will be many more births like ours in the future when people do their research and see the benefits of giving birth in a field surrounded by chanting alpacas.

Oh, you gave birth in a hospital? That might be why your baby doesn't sleep through the night. Did you try putting your baby's placenta under your pillow and eating only raw potato for the first three days after their birth?

Oh, you didn't? Well, that's just one thing that might have helped. We did it — but I mean, I think the reason why little Quinoa is such a good sleeper is because we talked to her about sleep. We told her she needs to sleep, and she just really respects us as her parents. And she's an old soul — she's very advanced. It's quite awkward for the other children in coffee group because little Quinoa is just so ahead of the pack. I really worry for her because sometimes children can be intimidated by her exceptional beauty and winning personality and superior intellect.

She is really good at tummy time. Which is awkward for us because we don't actually believe in tummy time. It's actually conceptually a real tool of fascism if you think about it.

Is that why yours won't sleep through? Tummy time?

tilts head to the side

That's a shame. You know they need to sleep for their development. It's, like, super really important.

Oh well, I'm sure it will happen eventually. Little Quinoa was a natural. We only did a few little things to help.

What were they? Well, we had a routine from pre-conception. Basically I created an aura of positivity and light around the pile of reeds and crystals that we placed the basket we made for her out of my heart-partner's chest hair on to. Then we chanted under the light of the red moon. I lactated early, so we bathed in my colostrum and just put all of our energy into what we call a sleep harvest.

Oh, a sleep harvest is a metaphor for the dreams we planted in our hope soil.

Are you using a white noise app?

Oh really? *tilts head to the side* We use organic white noise. We prefer not to expose her to chemical and unnatural white noise. Instead, each night I create a body symphony for Quinoa — Trent and I burp and break wind to the tune of 'Kumbaya'. We feel it really centres her.

Are you breastfeeding? I've found that things have gone really well for me now that I'm on a mainly grass diet. I have grass in the morning and at lunchtime and at night. Grass is paleo, so you're really safe using it as your main food group. But it really needs to be grass-fed grass.

Have you considered that maybe having a nursery could be the reason why your baby doesn't sleep? I always thought nurseries were quite oppressive in that they have four walls, generally. So we created a papier mâché cave for little Quinoa. We just created a paste from our sweat and urine and copies of *Naturally Parenting Naturally*, and we found that's a more inviting home for her.

Do you use blankets?

tilts head to the side

Oh, we don't. We just blow on her. Yes, all night. It seems a more respectful way to parent than using artificial sheets of thread.

I'm guessing you watch a lot of screens? No offence, but a parent who cares about their child wouldn't do that — but absolutely no judgement at all, friend!

I wonder if maybe you might feel more at peace with your parenting if you frolicked naked in the cool spring air instead of going to Junglerama?

We personally don't take little Quinoa to places like that because we feel it would be hurtful to her psyche to believe she is going to a jungle when actually it's just an indoor playground.

Instead I have created a playground for her myself out of Mason jars and bird song.

But you know, we all have to do what we have to do.

tilts head

We can't all be natural parents.

I THOUGHT I KNEW WHAT TYPE OF MOTHER I WOULD BE

Nothing breaks you apart and puts you together again like motherhood.

Sometimes I think the word 'motherhood' is too simple. We need a word to encompass what this really is. This thing that is redemptive. This thing that takes you to your absolute limit. It is destroying. But it is something you'd willingly do over and over again. This thing you'd never ever want to be without.

I thought I knew what type of mother I would be. But I had no idea.

On the one hand, I believed motherhood wouldn't change me. But then there were all of my fantasies about the type of mother I'd be. The daydreams I had. The imagining of my life *after* — they all featured a woman who wasn't anything like me.

I imagined I'd be calm and never frazzled. I'd lose all of my worrying thoughts. The way my mind almost always veered toward the catastrophic would no longer happen when I was a mother.

I'd laugh and I'd be patient. I'd be organised — something I'd never been. I imagined I'd always arrive on time to playdates and health appointments despite the fact that I've always been late.

I'd be good with money, because mums are good with money. I'd be selfless, because, above all, mothers are selfless. I wouldn't miss the time I used to have to myself. How could I? Every moment with my child would be a joy.

I was wrong, of course. But it wasn't a flashing lights, make sure everyone knows it, public *wrong*. It was a gentle hand on my shoulder saying 'You couldn't have known'.

And I am patient. And I'm often calm. But I am usually frazzled.

And that's OK.

I have worrying thoughts like I always did. My thoughts race towards catastrophe as often as they ever did.

But . . . being a mother made me realise I needed to get help to address that. I did this while carrying my baby. For some reason or another I never thought I was important enough to focus solely on my mental health. To try to address why I am so anxious so much of the time. My babies have taught me I do matter. I am important.

And I still have those thoughts. Some days are worse than others. But I don't take them lying down anymore. I don't allow them to engulf me. I take a deep breath and I fight and I say I'm not losing any more of my life to this. Because I matter to my children.

Being a mother has made me realise I'm far more capable than I thought I was, than I was made to believe I was.

And when my son was fighting for his life in hospital, I was strong. And I was capable. And I held it together just like every other mother in that ward.

Something about motherhood makes you tough while never keeping you tough. Never closing you off to your world. To your children. You're the most vulnerable you'll ever be, but you're unbreakable.

I have so many moments of selflessness, but I miss the time I had alone. Even while I'd never change a thing. Acknowledging the different aspects of my life then and now (and sometimes missing and even pining for the then) doesn't make me a bad mother — it makes me human.

Never before have I been so human.

Every moment isn't a joy — but my sons are always my joy. Some days it's hard to find joy, in amongst the sleep deprivation and the pull of trying to be a good mum, a good wife, a good friend, a good sister, a good daughter. But there is always, always joy.

So I might have been wrong, but it's never felt so right.

IS YOUR BABY GOING THROUGH A SLEEP REGRESSION?

∿

A good baby falls asleep immediately after birth. Generally, babies then sleep for six to 12 months. This is a hibernation period. If at any point they wake, it's likely they're having a sleep regression.

Here is your definitive guide to sleep regressions. It's important to be able to explain why your precious baby isn't sleeping all the time, so here is a handy list for you to match their age with their appropriate sleep regression. I've also provided some handy tips on how to address each sleep regression, so you'll be sleeping through the night in no time!

You can also use this list to provide helpful advice to other parents, like 'That sounds like the eight-month sleep regression' or 'That sounds like the nine-month sleep regression' or 'That sounds like the 11-month sleep regression.' Once you establish which sleep regression their child is going through, you should then add 'Think that's bad! Just wait until the x-month sleep regression!'

It is very helpful for parents to know that their child is having a sleep regression, and the only way they will know is if someone tells them. It's possible that the fact that they haven't slept in 72 hours will signal them that their child is having some kind of sleep regression, but really, it's a public service that you tell them as well. They definitely won't want to stab you many, many, many times.

FOUR-WEEK SLEEP REGRESSION

At around four weeks old your baby will have a sleep regression because they've come to realise they are no longer in the womb. It usually takes around four to six weeks for a baby to realise they're surrounded by air and not fluid. The best way to handle this regression is to make your home more womb-like. If it's at all possible, replace your door with a giant papier mâché vagina. Flood your house, grow gills and live as a fish hybrid.

FIVE-WEEK SLEEP REGRESSION

At around five weeks old your child will have a sleep regression because they have everything they need and they're bored and I mean, why not? What else are they going to do this week? They're too young to go clubbing. Simulate the clubbing environment at home by incorporating ecstasy and glowsticks into your bedtime routine.

SIX-WEEK SLEEP REGRESSION

At around six weeks old your baby will have a sleep regression because they have discovered sound. This sleep regression can be handled by playing music and not playing music and talking loudly while whispering very quietly — depending on what works for your baby. A good trick is to play music loudly and if your child goes to sleep then always play music forever for the rest of your life. If you play music loudly and they cry, then never ever listen to music again.

EIGHT-WEEK SLEEP REGRESSION

At around eight weeks old your baby will have a sleep regression because the equinox has unbalanced their aural waves. Summon the energy of the great crystal god Trevalanis, create a circle out of amber beads and stand in the middle of it, naked. Ignore your neighbours yelling at you to put some clothes on. They're not enlightened like you.

10-12-WEEK SLEEP REGRESSION

At around 10 to 12 weeks old your baby will have a sleep regression because they are trapped in a hysterical spiral of existential crisis. You must read the works of Ayn Rand to them while wearing ceremonial robes. Until they understand Objectivism they're just not going to get through this period.

FOUR-MONTH SLEEP REGRESSION

At around four months old your baby will suddenly realise that their buggy is second-hand. This will cause a sleep regression. There's not a great deal you can do regarding this sleep regression, but it should only last around four to 48 weeks.

FIVE-MONTH SLEEP REGRESSION

At five months old your baby will have a sleep regression because you put them in a Jolly Jumper even though that woman on the internet told you not to. You can't take it back and that's on you.

SIX-MONTH SLEEP REGRESSION

At around six months old your baby will have a sleep regression because they have discovered they have feet. In most regions in New Zealand it's not acceptable to surgically remove a child's feet, so it's best to just leave them, but you could cover them — say in a pair of socks or a blanket washed in the tears of a mother who hasn't slept in six months.

SEVEN-MONTH SLEEP REGRESSION

At around seven to 22 months old your baby will discover they don't actually need to sleep. With the power of Satan they're able to exist without rest. This is a special time, and you should Cherish Every Moment.

EIGHT-MONTH SLEEP REGRESSION

At around eight months old your baby will be eating solids. Which will cause a sleep regression. Although not feeding them will make them tired, it will also make them cranky. So sadly, this isn't the way to deal with this sleep regression. The best way to handle the eight months to two years sleep regression is to drink a lot of alcohol between the hours of 9 p.m. and 11.30 p.m.

NINE-MONTH SLEEP REGRESSION

At around nine months old your baby should be finished with the eight-month sleep regression, which carried on from the seven-month sleep regression. The nine-month sleep regression is just for fun, and it's a great way to carry you through to the 10-month sleep regression.

10-MONTH SLEEP REGRESSION

At around 10 months old your baby will be getting ready to turn one. As preparation for this they're going to continue to not sleep so they can also not sleep after their birthday. This is a way of reminding you that you're never going to sleep again. It's the most gentle sleep regression and is really just a gift from your child, who definitely isn't the personification of evil.

11-MONTH SLEEP REGRESSION

At around 11 months old your baby will have a growth spurt. They've been having growth spurts their whole lives, but inexplicably the growth spurt they have at 11 months is behind this sleep regression that is definitely a thing and not something someone on the internet made up. The best way to deal with this is to howl at the moon at 3 a.m. every night for eight nights.

12-MONTH SLEEP REGRESSION

At around 12 months old, your baby is a one-year-old! Isn't that magical? This causes a sleep regression, because of course it does.

13-16-MONTH SLEEP REGRESSION

From 13 to 16 months old your baby will have a sleep regression because they are committed to having sleep regressions.

17-19-MONTH SLEEP REGRESSION

Your baby is walking! Maybe. Whether they are walking or not, you're getting a sleep regression. Because waking up 6000 times a night helps them walk or something.

20-MONTH SLEEP REGRESSION

At 20 months old your child will have a sleep regression because you swaddled them when they were a baby. If you didn't swaddle them, they will also have a sleep regression. The best way to get through this sleep regression is to swaddle yourself.

21-MONTH SLEEP REGRESSION

At 21 months old your child will have a sleep regression because fuck you.

23-MONTH SLEEP REGRESSION

At 23 months old your child will have a sleep regression to protest the patriarchal gender norms that dictate our lives.

TWO-YEAR SLEEP REGRESSION

At two years old your child will have a sleep regression to celebrate two years of you never sleeping.

Congratulations! You made it two years! The good news is that you should only have 10–287 more sleep regressions until they're teenagers and refuse to get out of bed.

WE BUILT A VILLAGE

There's a lot of talk about a village, and how we don't have one anymore. How mothers before us knew it takes a village. That they spent their days at each other's houses, children happily playing outside as they laughed over cups of tea and ate home-made biscuits.

How they talked about everything and nothing and they had connection.

How their babies grew together. Learning how to walk as they leaned on each other.

How life was simpler back then.

Your village was small. But you could call on each other.

And someone would come over and clean your house if you rang and said you'd had a rough night, the baby is teething and you just can't stop crying.

And the mothers would come and they'd make you a good, strong cup of tea. And they'd put you to sleep and take the kids for a walk.

And they say we don't have that anymore. That life is too fast now. It's too complex. We don't have villages. We don't look out for each other.

There are so many column inches about the mummy wars and how we've labelled and separated ourselves from each other.

Not like back then when living next door was enough to build a friendship on nothing but the fact that the baby had a wail louder than a siren.

And they taught each other to feed their babies. And life was easy. It was different.

But we don't have that now, they say.

But it's strange. I hear this, but I am writing from within the village.

We didn't build a village with bricks.

We didn't lean over the back fence and say, 'Would you like a cuppa?'

We reached out and into a virtual world when we realised we were all going through the same thing.

We built a village not from mortar but from tweets and fuzzy words on a forum titled 'Why won't my baby sleep?'

We built friendships on nothing but the fact that our baby cries with such ferocity that it makes our head spin.

We taught each other that we were enough, no matter what anybody else said. It wasn't always easy. It was different.

We know it takes a village. As our children play, we laugh with friends no less real because we happen to chat online. We make plans to catch up at the park by instant message because we built this village through tapping out 'SOS' on a keyboard.

And the call was answered even across the seas, and our village is wide and open.

We talk about everything and nothing and we have connection.

Our babies grow together but apart, and we lean on each other as they learn to walk.

Life might not always feel simple, but we simply know that whatever happens we will have a kind word lighting up a page when we turn to our phones.

No matter the time. Or our location. We have this village.

We can call on each other and we rally. We create villages where there weren't any before.

We use labels to identify needs to ensure support. This place is a home for the mums who wait by hospital beds for babies that might not get better. This place is a home for mums whose children struggle with social interaction or whose minds never stop racing. This place is a home for the mums who feel so anxious so much of the time that we make sure we cheer the achievement of just leaving the house. This place is a home for the mums who never felt comfortable calling themselves mums. This place is a home for the mums who have grief raw and ragged at the surface. This place is a home for the mums who feel they're never quite good enough.

This is a safe village where there's a place for everyone.

And someone will start a thread where they share a bank account number so they can start collecting for the mum who needs her car fixed. She lost her job while on parental leave and her partner left.

They're a message away when you have a rough night, the baby is teething and you just can't stop crying.

And the mothers will come and they'll tell you that you need a good, strong cup of tea. And they'll say, 'I can't be with you to hold you tight, but I can promise you from here that you'll be OK, Mama.'

And they say we don't have that anymore. That life is too fast now. It's too complex. That we don't have villages. We don't look out for each other.

But I'm writing this from a village.

Where we always look out for each other.

THE CONFESSIONAL

eeee

It's time — time for some truth. Time for some parenting confessions.

I'll be honest, I have told a few white lies in the past, at a coffee group, to a colleague, a friend even . . . definitely to family now and then. It's just sometimes I don't want the lecture or the raised eyebrow or the tilt of the head and the half-smile. I am sure every parent has a confession or two. This will be our safe place. I'll share if you do . . .

deep breath

CONFESSION #1: WE ARE CO-SLEEPERS.

Look, I try to pretend we aren't. But we are. I will say things like 'Oh he mostly sleeps in his own bed' or 'It's mostly just a visit in the morning to get him to sleep longer.' Unless if by 'mostly' I actually mean 'never', it's a fib. Because mostly he actually never bloody sleeps unless one of us is in there with him.

We never set out to be co-sleepers. I actually said before having kids that I'd never co-sleep. My bed is a sanctuary, I said. Ha ha *sob*. For my hubris, my bed is now not a sanctuary. Co-sleeping is the only way my youngest sleeps for longer than 45 minutes. He will cry out and reach out a hand into the darkness, and when he touches my shoulder or my husband's wrist or the side of my face his body relaxes and he goes back to sleep. If he reaches out and we are not there, he screams and wakes himself up and then it takes forever to get him to go back to sleep. That is why we co-sleep.

I've talked about co-sleeping, but I've often told people it's only occasionally, or I've allowed them to believe that our youngest has grown out of it. We recently went on holiday and I didn't put up the cot. That's when I realised we are really co-sleepers. I didn't even bother with *pretending* that he was going to sleep in the cot at any point.

I should be more open about this, but lots of people who don't co-sleep believe co-sleeping is *why* he won't sleep. I co-slept with Eddie until he was almost two, and then he moved into his own bed in his own room, just before Ham arrived. Eddie is a great sleeper now, and he even has sleepovers. Co-sleeping (I believe) has worked really well for him, and we are sure it will work out well for Ham, too. So because I don't want to be told to not do it, because I'm comfortable with doing it, I usually tell people he doesn't sleep with us — but the cat is out of the bag now, I guess.

Also, people ask weird questions about co-sleeping. Like when I once said I co-slept with Eddie I got asked, 'But what about . . . y'know . . .' And I'm like, sex? And they were like 'Yeah, y'know.' I was literally six months' pregnant when they asked me this question.

CONFESSION #2: I AM NOT OK WITH MY KID NOT SLEEPING THROUGH THE NIGHT.

I so often tell people I am OK with not ever getting sleep. I always say things like 'Yeah, I've accepted that Ham is just not a good sleeper.' I have not. I am really fucking upset about having two babies who don't sleep.

There, I said it. It's bullshit and it's not fair and I want a baby who sleeps. Damn, that felt good! I tell people all the time that it's just the way it is and I'm all right with it. NOPE.

The other day I saw one of those pictures on Instagram — you know one of those typography things, some baby book milestone app thing. The baby was sleeping and it had the baby's name and weight typed over it all pretty, and under 'interests' it said something like pottery and fascism (I can't remember) and it also said 'Sleeping through the night at eight weeks' and for a brief second — actually not that brief — I saw this red mist. Is that weird? I wanted to kind of punch a wall. That's not weird, right? Don't answer that.

I honestly am so fucking annoyed that my kids don't sleep and that I've tried everything and just *this is it*. And I'm so fucking annoyed other people get two or three kids who sleep all fucking night from *two fucking months old*. WHAT THE FUCK! And sometimes I see those posts where people are all *Oh I'm so bored my baby has been sleeping for a week and a half and I just want to wake him up!* And for a second I actually put a hex on them. Not a really bad curse. I just silently pray that they will pour some cereal into a bowl and then pour the milk but only a tiny bit will come out and the carton will be empty and it will be too much milk to save the cereal but not enough milk to eat it. Or I wish that they will go to the store and their favourite brand of cereal will be temporarily out of stock. (Yes, my spells are mostly breakfast-related — don't judge me.)

I feel real sadness that I won't ever know what it's like to parent without being severely sleep-deprived. I really wish I knew what it was like. I wish I knew what type of mother I would be without bags under my eyes and a dull headache. Would I be calmer? More patient? Would I be a much better mother than I am? Would I be a better wife, a better daughter, sister, and friend? Would I be a better volunteer, a better community member, a better writer?

I feel sad. And so I lie. I say I'm not that tired and I say I am fine with the fact that my kids don't sleep. I am convincing myself so that I can adjust to my reality and eventually, hopefully, make peace with it.

CONFESSION #3: WE DON'T EVER EAT AS A FAMILY AND I DON'T GIVE A SHIT.

And yes, I'm always going to lie and say we do. I get it, eating as a family is important. Yes. Fine. I concede this is true. But it is also significantly more stressful than not eating as a family for us right now.

The baby eats first, in a high-chair. Our dining-room table is covered in 128 loads of washing. My oldest does not eat with any kind of distraction. He would love it if we sat together, encouraging conversation. Because then he could talk and not eat.

Look, I've seen that ad. I've seen where they ask the kids who they want to eat with and they're all 'Mummy and Dadda' and that's cute, but also I don't care. Logistically I need to eat my food quickly so I can handle the youngest who just threw an entire pot of yoghurt on the floor while my husband coaches our son, saying, 'Just one more spoonful please, buddy.' We are working on ways to make dinnertime less stressful, but right now this segmented regime of splitting up the children and assigning one adult to each one to make sure they both have something in their bellies before bedtime works and is the least stressful way to eat.

Yet I will always tell people we eat as a family, because we do — umm, sort of. I mean, I eat the bits left over on their plates or the parts Eddie doesn't want while standing and trying to catch falling food (which I also eat). So we do kind of eat as a family.

I get why people who have grown kids are always like 'eat together at the dinner table blah blah blah'. I mean, they have fond memories that are very removed from the realities of having two under three, because they're reflecting on something they did 20 years ago. Also, they're all about conversations at the table, as if the table is some designated talk-zone and nowhere else in the house is a place where you can talk.

We have our conversations before bed. Snuggled up warm. Sleepy, tired eyes closing as we recount the day. Free from distraction, we talk about who we helped that day. How we can help others tomorrow. What our favourite part of the day was. Who was our best friend today? Who loves us? Who makes us happy? Can there ever be a dolphin that is also a firefighter, and do dinosaurs smile, and what would happen if you didn't have a face (what is it with the weird shit kids come up with?)? It is relaxed and loving and gentle and it doesn't feel forced.

Eventually those conversations will move to the dinner table, but the fact is dinner right now for us is just getting the first-born to eat and stopping the second-born from eating everything. So rest assured, not only are we talking but the oldest is very rarely not talking.

But all of that feels like justification for something I don't feel guilty about, so instead I just say, 'Mmm yeah eating at the table so important yup definitely . . .'

So there you go. My confessions. Maybe you think I'm silly for not just being out with them — and you're kind of right, which is why I'm putting them out there. We are our own worst judges, and even though I don't feel guilty about any of these . . . maybe I do? Maybe it still feels like I have a picture in my head of what a good mother is and I'm still trying to be that image.

Maybe it's time to put pencil to paper and redefine her. Draw her so she looks a little bit more like me, so I can be a little kinder to myself.

WHISPER FIGHTING

Prior to having children I might have been one of those insufferable people who said 'My partner and I never argue.' It was basically a lie then, but it's the biggest lie now. Nothing makes you fight about everything as much as having kids does.

It's a very bizarre thing that I feel closer than ever to my husband since we had children — I love him even more than I did before kids — but we bicker *so much more* since we became parents.

The extreme sleep deprivation that comes with small children is basically like dynamite to a relationship. Nothing encourages seething rage and fury and righteous anger more than trying to survive a day on a few hours of broken sleep.

You can't take your exhaustion out on your kids (that's frowned upon) so it's often the partner who cops it.

It was only after kids I realised there's a thing called Whisper Fighting. Whisper Fighting is when the kids are asleep and you're angry but you don't want to wake them.

So you engage in a full-blown fight, but only in whispers. You make up for your inability to yell by gesticulating furiously and hysterically.

Theatrical silent screaming and over-the-top sighing is a large part of Whisper Fighting.

Whisper Fights are known for being comically short, as they often happen at 3 a.m. and you don't want to waste any *time that you could spend sleeping*. They're usually over within five minutes.

They usually end the same way:

'LOOK I'M TIRED. OK!'

'I'M TIRED TOO!'

'I'M SORRY ALL RIGHT. FUCK.'

'I'M SORRY TOO OK. FUCK.'

A gentle acceptance that you're both frayed and falling apart at the seams is a large part of post-baby relationships. That you now have a new person in your life that you love even more than you love each other is a big deal. It's something to navigate. And without a road map.

Obviously I'm not going to give relationship advice, but I will say this: never say 'Calm down', because nobody has ever calmed down when they've been told to calm down. Never wake the baby with an argument. And say sorry when the rage you're feeling is at the universe for not letting you sleep and not your partner. Whisper 'sorry'. As a gesture, it's louder than you think.

A WHOLE NIGHT

He slept through the night.

For the first time, since he was born, he slept longer than four hours. Four hours was his previous achievement. And that four hours? Incredible. Indescribable.

But a night? A whole night?

When he woke, he popped up his fuzzy little head. He rubbed his eyes with his tiny little fists. A look of wonder rushed across his fat little face. Even he was surprised he'd managed to sleep. All night.

My husband and I woke disorientated and comically bewildered. How could it be morning? We were due at least three to six wake-ups over the seven hours we class as 'night-time' slash 'lose all hope and will to live time'.

The Ham giggled. He flung himself backwards onto the bed and dissolved into fat, ridiculous chuckles that turned into absurdly loud shrieks of laughter, while we stared in amazement until we all gave in and fell into the moment, too. All of us howling, tears pulling at my eyes as I pulled the battery from my phone — surely the time was wrong. My husband peered out the window: 'It's morning?'

A beautiful smile.

The Ham had finally achieved what we thought was the unachievable. It had taken him 13 months. And oh, those 13 months, waking every 45 minutes, screaming for hours while we rocked and sang and hissed and cried and cried. There were torn nipples. Whispered fights: 'IT'S YOUR TURN!' Sleep apps that we had to stop using because I couldn't handle my day knowing for sure that I'd had only two hours and 45 minutes' — broken, so very broken — sleep. There were moments when I really wondered what the hell I had done to deserve a child that hated sleep. In my worst moments — those 4 a.m. desperate moments when you know your other child will be up soon, and you *still* haven't slept — I thought about running away. Far away.

How can we, how did we, how do we, keep doing this? Day in? Day out? Each night I felt as if I was staring out at the sea from a steep and ragged cliff-top. I felt so lost. So guilty. So confused. There were some nights where I cried buckets even before I climbed exhausted into bed.

I have never, in my entire life, even in my first-born's first year, wanted sleep as much as I wanted it near the end of this 13 months. Needed it. Desperately. I would have traded anything. Anything.

I had begun to feel like I was fraying at the edges. Little bits of me kept catching on things and I was becoming less of myself every day.

Sleep deprivation does that. It steals from you, but you don't notice at first. You're surprised by how well you're coping. You make comments about how it's amazing that you are getting by and *doing so much*.

But you catch yourself running into the kitchen and you can't remember what you went there for. Or you get home from the supermarket and you've forgotten the one thing you needed. They're the little things. You laugh them off.

But then it's the bigger things. You start to feel as if you're living in a fog. You retreat. You keep getting sick. You hurt a lot. Your bones and your heart. In the evening, you find yourself sitting down for a minute to collect yourself, but then you look at the time and you've been in that one spot, staring at the wall, for almost an hour.

You don't know where time goes. But every moment is waking.

I have been accused of being melodramatic about sleep. Told parenting is *tiring*. Why did I have children if I couldn't cope with a change in sleeping patterns?

There's no point trying to get someone to understand the sleep deprivation many parents experience with their child in that first year, or more. There's no point.

You know or you don't know. Some people are blessed with babies who sleep 10 (sometimes even more) hours a night. For most of my son's life I have lived on around 20 hours sleep *a week*. Sometimes more, usually less.

This is not unusual.

People like to pretend it is. It makes them uncomfortable, so they suggest it's not really happening. If it is, it's the fault of the mother. She's not trying hard enough to get her baby to sleep. She's not having naps. She needs to put herself first. She's not practising self-care. She's a martyr.

All of the judgements and assumptions and ignorant comments sit at the bottom of a cliff. Above are countless mothers who stand and face the roaring waves each night and say:

This will pass
We are doing the best we can
Tonight might be different
Tomorrow is another day
We are doing the best we can
It won't always be like this.

And it won't. And when I'm on that cliff-top, I'm not alone. And neither are you. This chorus in the night is one we share. We are together alone in this. It won't always be like this and we will get there together.

One night you will kiss your baby's sweet little face —

expectant and full. A little moon peering out in the darkness. You will kiss them and silently wish . . . or maybe you'll be too tired even for that. You'll fall into sleep — maybe easily, maybe it'll take a while.

And you'll wake up in the morning after they've slept all night.

Hours of blissful sleep that will sustain you until it happens again.

You've got this, mama. You're not alone on the cliff-top. You'll make it. I know you will.

THE IN-MY-DAY COMMITTEE

MINUTES OF THE IN-MY-DAY COMMITTEE

25 November 2015

In attendance: Gladys, who had eight children and didn't breastfeed any of them and they turned out fine; John, who thinks mothers these days have no decorum; Prudence, whose children slept through the night from birth; Doris, who has a granddaughter who called her daughter Charlie even though Charlie is clearly a name for a boy; and Ernest, who thinks Charlie is going to grow up confused.

Apologies: Betty couldn't make it as she needs to spend her lunch hour telling a young mum at a bus stop that her baby needs to be on solids because it's 'wasting away'.

Meeting of the In-My-Day Committee is now in session.
John begins the meeting by stating that PC has indeed gone mad because he saw a woman at the pool who was breastfeeding a child right there at the pool.

Clarification was sought as to the age of the child.

Agreement by Committee that actually it doesn't matter. No children should be publicly breastfed.

'It should be in the home and that's that.' Vigorous head-nodding.

Break for tea.

Gladys would like it on the record once again that she never breastfed any of her eight children and they turned out just fine.

Point of order by Doris that there weren't lactation consultants back then and you just got on with it, didn't you?

Agreement from Committee that indeed their generation just got on with it and that's entirely what's wrong with this generation. They just won't get on with it.

Forty-seven-minute discussion about how there wasn't anyone to help you In-My-Day. Agreement once again that PC has indeed gone mad.

Break for tea.

Interjection that everything has gone to hell in a hand-basket, as evidenced by mothers working outside the home.

Prudence asks for silence so that she can spend two and a half hours talking about how she had 12 hours sleep a night In-My-Day because babies weren't coddled so they slept through the night from conception.

General uproar over the word 'coddled'. Furious and violent agreement that children today are coddled.

Agreement that all babies slept through the night from pre-conception In-My-Day and that mothers these days don't know how lucky they are.

Ernest wakes to agree that mothers these days don't know how lucky they are.

Break for tea.

Doris notes that you had no choice but to breastfeed 'In-My-Day' because there was no such thing as formula. Rousing agreement from the committee that mothers these days should be grateful that they have a choice.

'I had no choice but to breastfeed. All children were breastfed In-My-Day and they turned out fine,' repeats Doris for around 90 minutes. 'And we didn't make a fuss, when we were out and about we fed where we needed to and nobody made a fuss!'

Ernest wakes to point out that the very problem is choice. Mothers nowadays choose work when In-My-Day they knew their role was to look after the children. And they're entitled, too. They always make a fuss.

Kerfuffle as John puts his back out because he so enthusiastically agrees with the sentiment that mothers once knew their role and were not entitled and didn't make fusses.

Prudence agrees that she never had a challenging moment in her time caring for her children, she enjoyed every second, cherished every moment, loved every day and had no difficulty whatsoever at any point. Agreement that her daughter-in-law is not cut out to be a mother.

Eighty-seven-minute discussion about how her daughter-in-law is lazy for not returning to work and for making Prudence's son move to Melbourne for a job. Prudence never sees Theodore or her precious grandson (some time is spent trying to remember grandson's name — says it is 'one of those new age names like MoonBubble') and they won't let her visit as often as she wants to.

Last time she went over the house was filthy and she had to say that, didn't she? The baby had just been born, but that's no excuse.

Agreement from the Committee that that is indeed no excuse.

Agreement from Committee that she had to say that.

Doris would like it on record that she was vacuuming hours after her son Clarry was born.

Discussion that grandparents have rights, too, you know. Also that In-My-Day you were house-proud.

Agreement that today's generation isn't house-proud.

Doris would like to discuss the need for solids from three weeks old. Agreement that babies these days are underweight. General discussion regarding which foods are best 'firsts'. Noted that John's son was overreacting when John gave his grandson a Werther's Original when he was five days old.

Prudence remembers her grandson's name — it is Leif. This begins three-hour discussion on how children these days have ridiculous names and how In-My-Day you had three names to pick from: Tom, Ben and Bill if you had a boy, and Mary, Ann and Helen if you had a girl.

Agreement that Doris naming her daughter Ethel is quite different because that's a lovely name. And so is Cyril. Motion passed that Cyril be recognised as a Proud Name.

Discussion about Doris's granddaughter Charlie being named Charlie becomes quite heated.

Full and rowdy agreement that children born today are confused.

On-record statements from eight-day discussion on how children born today are confused:

* Boys shouldn't wear pink.
* Girls need to wear pink.
* It should not be difficult for Doris to be able to tell if a baby is a boy or a girl.
* Adam and Eve not Adam and Steve.
* Women today don't know how to knit.
* Whatever happened to the name John? Now that's a strong boy's name.
* It's illegal to be a man.
* What about that chap who had to say sorry for being a man?
* Feminism is to blame for most of society's ills.
* It's absolutely fair that Doris refuses to call her

granddaughter Charlie and instead calls her Charlotte.

* Girls want to play with dolls — that's biology, says
  John, who left school at nine, unlike young people these
  days who study at the taxpayers' expense.

Unanimous 'Well I never' by the group as Gladys reveals she saw a boy with painted nails at the bus stop.

Twenty-eight minutes of 'not In-My-Day' repeated.

Break for tea.

Suggestion by Gladys that she must get home in order to visit her newest great-grandchild is met with excitement by the Committee.

Discussion of what Gladys's granddaughter was like during her pregnancy lasts around 45 minutes.

She complained a lot even though pregnancy isn't an illness. Gladys says she lost half of her body weight, but she could stand to lose that much according to Doris.

Doris reminds Committee she had 18 children. One after the other. And never complained once. In fact she's never complained even once in her whole life.

Because In-My-Day we just got on with it. That's the problem with this generation — they just don't get on with it.

Not like In-My-Day . . .

HAPPY MOTHER'S DAY

eeee

What do we want for Mother's Day? How about an end to annoying things people say to mothers for just one day?

Here is a by-no-means-exhaustive list of things people need to stop saying to mothers of little ones:

CHERISH EVERY MOMENT! / THEY GROW UP SO FAST! / ENJOY IT WHILE IT LASTS!

Guess what? Mothers are acutely aware that their children grow up. They literally watch them doing exactly that all of their lives. And it breaks their hearts a lot of the time, because there's a constant push and pull going on.

It's a beautiful tragedy that your aim as mother is to empower and prepare the person you love the most in life to one day leave your home. Like all mothers, I love my kids so much it hurts, and each day that passes they become less dependent on me and it's so sad. One day they're going to leave home (and me). One day they might move to another country — a country that I'm not in.

I really do not want to focus on that part of the job right now! I want to focus on the fact that I now have slightly more time to think about who I am in the context of being their mum. And also I can drink wine now. That's a good thing, isn't it? Let mums do that without policing every stage of parenting they go through.

Needlessly and relentlessly reinforcing the fact that babies will grow up (and you'll be sorry!) isn't helpful. We can't do anything about it and this EVERY SECOND THEY ARE GETTING BIGGER AND

YOU WILL NEVER HAVE THIS MOMENT AGAIN / KEEP YOUR EYES OPEN / WATCH THEM. THEY ARE GROWING / ONCE A MOMENT IS GONE. IT IS GONE FOREVER thing is weird and unnecessary.

The people who say 'Cherish every moment' didn't cherish every moment.

No parent cherishes every moment, because every moment isn't worth cherishing. It just isn't. I refuse, absolutely refuse, to cherish the moment when I discovered a small nugget of poo in the laundry pile. I refuse. I didn't know what it was and I picked it up and I was so tired that I rubbed it in my hand to see what it was.

I rubbed a poo nugget into my hand.

That is not a moment to cherish.

Does that mean I don't cherish all the actually cherishable moments? No, it doesn't.

Cherish away if you want. But it's not compulsory, and it doesn't make you any less of a mum if some days you cherish the moment they go to sleep and you get to drink an entire glass of wine in 30 seconds.

Hollow slogans that just inspire guilt are pointless. Every mother loves their baby more than anything. Every parent thinks their child is everything right in the world. Everyone loves their kids — it's the loving the kids that matters, not the loving of all of the moments.

Also — 'enjoy it while it lasts' is weirdly cruel. Like, how about just enjoy being alive while it lasts. One day you'll be dead. You'll be burnt or your body will be put into the ground and worms will have sex in your face.

This is why nobody invites me out anymore.

HAVE YOU TRIED USING WHITE NOISE / A VAPOURISER / A SLEEP SACK / SEEING A SLEEP CONSULTANT / THE CRY-IT-OUT METHOD / AN OSTEO-NATURO-CHIRO-PALEO-PATH / EATING HALF A

CAKE AND RUBBING THE OTHER HALF ON YOUR NAKED BODY AS A GIFT TO THE SLEEP GODS?

Have you tried shoving your unsolicited advice up your ass? Is that a thing that you've tried? Because I heard that really works.

I know you're trying to help, but if a mum wants your advice, she'll ask for it. If she doesn't ask for it, chances are that she doesn't want it.

PARENTS THESE DAYS . . . / IN MY DAY . . .

Shhhhhhh! Nothing good comes after 'Parents these days . . .' or 'In my day . . .'. Nothing! Just don't. I know in your day parents didn't take as many pictures as parents do today, but maybe that's because in your day a picture took 800 hours because someone had to chisel it into a cave wall. Things are different now. Some things are better. Some aren't. And it's all subjective. And nobody is going to feel better coming up with a comprehensive list of what's better or worse.

ANY TYPE OF NEGATIVE COMMENTARY ON SCREEN TIME

It's *so boring*. So you don't want my kid to watch *Fireman Sam*. Fine. Come over and entertain him then while I do 19,673 loads of washing. Go make a floral arrangement out of hopes and dreams and recycled yoga pants. Piss in a Mason jar and call it art. *Be my guest.*

ARE YOU GOING BACK TO WORK?

Are you? Are you working right now? What business is it of yours? Why do you care what I've chosen to do? I'd have volunteered this information if I wanted you to know. I'd have raised it as a topic of conversation if I wanted to discuss it. What I'm doing is work. So suck it.

DO YOU MISS YOUR BABY WHEN YOU'RE AT WORK?

Yes! And no! And maybe! And often! There's literally no way to answer this. And if a mother didn't *choose* to return to work it can be really painful to answer. And even mothers who do want to return to work find it difficult to answer. Maybe they do, but that doesn't change the choices they have or don't have. Maybe they don't, but they don't want to say that because of how people often react to a statement like 'Actually, I love pooping by myself'.

Which leads me to one I got last week:

OH, ARE YOU GOING TO MISS THEM WHEN YOU GO AWAY FOR A FEW DAYS?

I will be sleeping. That thing I haven't done in two years. So no. Probably not. Do fathers ever get asked this? Ever? I'm sure they don't . . . And you know what? I probably will miss them. But I am also going to get real drunk and dance to Beyoncé and not miss them at all.

YOU WANTED TO BE A PARENT!

Yes, I did. Did you want to be an asshole?

Wanting to be a parent has zero correlation with how challenging and isolating parenting can be sometimes. It's such an incredibly heartless thing to say: 'That's what you signed up for!'

Allow some complexity in that tiny little head of yours. Parenting isn't something you endure or barely survive any more than it's a constant and unyielding joy. It's wonderful and relentless. And, like the best things in life, it's really, really hard a lot of the time. I find this such an odd comment. Of all of the comments, it's the most profoundly weird and rude one, I reckon.

ARE YOU GOING TO HAVE ANOTHER ONE? / ARE YOU HOPING FOR A GIRL/BOY?

Get out of my uterus.

I am hoping for six hours' sleep — now be quiet.

DONT YOU THINK HE'S A BIT OLD TO WEAR A TUTU? ARENT YOU A BIT WORRIED HE'LL—

STOP. I WILL DESTROY YOU IF YOU SPEAK ANY MORE WORDS.

WHEN WILL YOU HAVE YOUR OWN KIDS? (TO STEP-MOTHERS AND STEP-FATHERS)

I have a lot of friends who are step-parents. I have been there when people have said this to them and it infuriates me. Being a parent is being there. Always. The good and bad. Friends of mine have been there through it all and put up with some really challenging circumstances. They're parents. End of story.

Being a parent is so much more than giving birth or providing DNA, and often it's not even that. It's like that cheesy-as-all-hell magnet: 'Anyone can be a father, it takes someone special to be a daddy.'

But not like daddy in a sex way. Daddy as in . . . OMG, I killed it, didn't I? I killed the nice moment we were having.

DONT YOU GET BORED BEING HOME ALL DAY?

No. Ever since I created a robot to take care of my children, my mind has been pretty focused on world peace, TBH. I've also been working on an 80,000-piece puzzle of twelfth-century France, so actually I'm making use of all this endless, relaxing time I have while caring for two kids under three.

Honestly, what do you think my kids do all day? Sleep? THAT IS NOT A THING THAT THEY DO.

IS HE A GOOD BABY?

No. He runs a Donald Trump fan page on Facebook and he keeps telling me he will sleep when he makes America great again. I thought maybe it was caused by teething?

WAIT UNTIL THEY'RE SCHOOL-AGED! / WAIT UNTIL THEY'RE PRE-TEENS! / WAIT UNTIL THEY'RE TEENAGERS!

Wait until death's sweet release! Honestly, it's such a weird thing that only seems to happen with parenting. If you ever say something is hard about the stage you're in, it's the law of physics or something that someone will leap out from behind a bush and scream 'Wait until they're . . .'

Where else does this happen? If someone says work is hard, people don't say 'Wait until your next job, it's going to fucking suck, mate!'

YOU'VE LOST THE BABY WEIGHT! / ARE YOU GOING TO LOSE THE BABY WEIGHT?

Shut up. I lost 10 pounds of it overnight. And if you fuck off out of my sight I'll have lost another 150 pounds.

YOU'RE SO LUCKY YOUR HUSBAND HELPS! / IS YOUR HUSBAND BABYSITTING? / IT'S SO GREAT HE'S INVOLVED!

HE IS THE CHILD'S PARENT. HE IS LITERALLY THE OTHER PARENT. IT IS LITERALLY HIS JOB LIKE IT IS MY JOB.

SLEEP WHEN THE BABY SLEEPS / HE MUST BE HUNGRY!

I'll actually kill you. I will.

★

So what *should* you say?
How about 'Happy Mother's Day! I hope you get a nap and if you don't I hope you get sleep tonight! I hope your kids eat.

I hope nobody puts anything in the toilet that isn't something that's meant to go in the toilet. I hope your day is full of wet sloppy kisses from gummy little mouths and little hands wrapped around your neck giving big, big cuddles. I hope your day is full of hand-drawn cards with smiling faces and vouchers for massages or new slippers or pretty flowers. I hope your day is full of love! I hope you get to relax a little. I hope you know you're everything to your children. That you're a good mum. That your family loves you and recognises the hard work that you do. I hope you get wine if you like wine, and chocolate (everybody likes chocolate, right?). I hope you get to put your feet up. Even if it's just for one day.'

What should you say to a new mum? Say 'You got this, mama. You know what you're doing, and if you don't — you'll get there. So I have no advice for you. I just want to talk about whatever you want. I want to screech with laughter with you. Look at photos of your kids on your phone. Celebrate the years you've been raising your precious wee ones. Congratulate you on keeping them home fires burning while not making any comment about those times the curtains almost caught fire.' I want to say I'm glad you got here — I'm glad that you're celebrating Mother's Day as a mum.

And if you're a mum of a child in hospital right now, I want to say I hope today is kind to you. I hope feeds go well, that you get to hold your baby in your arms. That you get good coffee. That you feel a moment of peace in a place not known for peace.

And if you are mourning your mum on Mother's Day, I want to say I'm sorry this day is so hard for you. That your mum would be proud of you. That this day feels lonely when your mother is no longer here, but your babies will look at you the way your mum once also looked at you. I hope you find comfort in your children. And if you don't have children I hope you find comfort in family and friends and loved ones.

If you don't have a mum who is able to parent you, I want to say good on you for breaking that cycle and for being the mother you deserved to have. For being better or trying to be better every day even when you're not sure what better looks like because you've never seen it. You're healing yourself even without knowing it. Mothering is redemptive and you're a great mum.

If you're a mum who has lost a child, I wish I had words for you. But none of us do. We can just say that our arms are always open to you. That you are in the hearts of all mothers. That we all hope this day doesn't bring you more pain.

If you're a mum parenting alone, know that on Mother's Day and all days we salute you for working your ass off for your whānau. What a great example to your children — showing them how you have so much love, more than enough despite there only being one of you. I hope your chosen family, the ones who are there for you, rally around you and give you the relaxing time you deserve on Mother's Day.

If you're a mum who is struggling to conceive or who has lost babies before they were born, this place is a home for you, too, and that pain is something you're not alone in. I hope next Mother's Day is different for you. Mothers everywhere are hoping you have your month where you see two lines. That you have that scan that says it'll be OK. That you'll hold your baby in your arms. That you get that first Mother's Day card that calls you by your new name — Mama.

Love to all of the mamas on Mother's Day. Wherever you are — have a lovely day.

DEAR INDOOR PLAYGROUND STAFF

I truly love you. I know your job isn't great. That you have to deal with constant screaming (mostly the kids). And parents who believe that paying a ludicrously inflated price for a playground that almost definitely has traces of gastroenteritis in the ball pit means that they don't have to parent their children on the premises.

I know this because I'm one of those parents.

And I appreciate you not judging me for it. I appreciate you taking my money and then steadfastly ignoring my terrible parenting in exchange.

When I say to my son who has taken his socks off for the eighteenth time:

Put your socks back on.

No, I said put your socks back on now.

Now.

What did I say?

What did I say?

What did I say?

What did I say?

What did I say?

You just mind your own business, clearing the table next to mine.

As I read a Janet Lansbury article on my phone about how you shouldn't say to children 'What did I say?,' you don't judge me.

You don't judge me as I say to myself: Janet Lansbury is so right. I am definitely going to change the way I talk to my child.

You don't judge me when I then say to my son literally eight seconds later:

Where are your socks?

I said you have to wear socks!

What did I say?

What did I say?

What did I say?

What did I say?

What did I say?

When I buy my second coffee in an hour and then thank you a little bit too intensely for it, you don't seem to mind.

You smile as I go back to reading the Janet Lansbury article about being present.

When I say to my child 'I'm not allowed in the playground, that lady said so' and point to you, you smile and nod. And I love you for it. In that moment, I love you more than I love my first-born who has just TAKEN HIS DAMN SOCKS OFF AGAIN.

Thank you for not telling me my son needs to wear socks. I don't know why he will wear socks literally everywhere except the one place he needs to wear socks.

Thank you, staff at the indoor playground, for not saying anything when that lady pointed to my 18-month-old baby and said, 'He needs to learn to share' and I said, 'That's not my baby, sorry.'

I know you know it's my baby. But fuck her, I just want a coffee in peace and she's a great-great-grandmother who hasn't parented in 800 years and has forgotten that children hate sharing so much they will literally snatch half-chewed food from the mouths of their parents.

Thank you for not judging me that time I fell asleep in the corner of the jumping castle.

Thank you for recognising that I truly believe that indoor playgrounds operate under the rules of Sparta. They go in as babies and come out as warriors.

What happens in the ball pit stays in the ball pit.

If my son breaks his leg it will be unfortunate, but it won't be your fault. You have given me relative peace for at least six, sometimes seven minutes at a time. And average, overpriced coffee. But mainly — you haven't judged my bad parenting.

You know indoor playgrounds are the home of bad parenting and you accept it.

Thank you for accepting me.

HOW TO BE KIND

Today was kind of a wonderful day. We had a Christmas party for our little charity Ballet is for Everyone. Lots of kids and parents and volunteers and friends came, and it was beautiful. Ballet is for Everyone is a wee thing a friend and I and Twitter started that provides free ballet classes for children. It's completely volunteer-run and everything is paid for by donations. It feels like every single person who has donated or volunteered has a different reason for why they support it. Personally, I wanted to do something because my son wanted to wear a tutu and I couldn't afford to put him in classes and I didn't know if I even wanted him in traditional classes even if I could afford them, and putting children who have or have had health problems into mainstream classes is really stressful anyway . . .

So, on a whim, we all decided to do this thing. And this thing turned into a thing that took over my life. And today we had our final classes for the year.

And throughout the party everyone there just kind of kept catching looks across the dancing children and grinning and clasping hands and just thinking: Look at this! Look at all these happy kids!

For five or so months we've put on classes every single weekend and children have had free classes and free ballet gear and tutus and all of these *things*. But I think the thing that they love the most is that they have all of these adults just totally invested in them as little people. They walk into the studio and the kids know it's all about them. It's like a birthday party — if it's your birthday, you're the special guest. But here, all of the kids are. Every Sunday. They know that nothing is expected of them. We — the adults — are here to assist them in just being the incredible little beings that they are.

Actually, they don't need any assistance in that regard. We basically just give them water when they say they're thirsty, ha!

And I've come to realise that this way of being around children is so life-affirming for them. So much of Eddie's confidence I attribute to the ballet 'lessons'. Our little discussions before bed on Sundays always involve talk of ballet, and tonight was no different.

But he did ask an interesting question and his answer to his question sparked off so many thoughts for me, here I am writing about them in a garbled, please-forgive-me-it's-Sunday type of way . . .

We were talking about ballet and how nice it was that we had so many different teachers today (we've had can-can dancers, a hula dancer, contemporary dancers and a belly dancer), and Eddie asked, 'Why did they come?'

And I thought it was a fairly straightforward question, but then I couldn't quite work out how to answer it. So I said, 'Why do you think they came?' And he said, 'Because they love all of us?'

And I thought, well yes. Why not? And then before I could work out what I should say, he said, 'It's nice they all love all of us because when they do love all of us it makes me feel kind.'

And I thought, well. Kids are pretty-very-extremely smart. Because he basically just told me how to teach him something I've pondered since the day I got pregnant.

How do we teach our kids to be kind?

Of all of the traits I want my children to have, kindness is my number one. I don't want Eddie to make a million dollars (though it would be nice), or be a champion athlete or award-winning author (though, sure, it'd be nice), or to have great fame or accolades — I want him to be kind.

I have read many things on how to encourage kindness. Gratitude. Empathy. So often it turns into a 'how to have good manners' screed, or it feels very complicated for something that seems like it shouldn't be complicated.

This evening, I kind of realised that it's just like anything else — we make sure they feel safe and loved and we model behaviour. It's pretty clear that when we are kind to all children, not just our children, when we let them just be the wonderful little freaks that they are — we are teaching kindness.

And of course this is the case. I mean, when I feel judged or belittled or when I am made to feel like I have to put on an act for others, I feel deeply resentful. When I feel excluded, or like I don't belong, I struggle to have any feeling of warmth toward anyone. A community is so inextricably linked to kindness — it's impossible to have one without the other. So of course, without community, without feeling unconditionally accepted, no wonder we struggle to be kind. Why should children be any different?

I know this is no great epiphany, but it made me have a lot of feelings. It was one of those rare moments in parenting when you think, maybe I'm not screwing them up for life. Maybe I am on the right track. These are the moments that sustain you through the hard bits, the 'how can I honestly be an adult right now and yet still be totally incapable of getting a baby out of a fluffing swaddle?' bits. When you stumble upon a parenting win, through no real effort on your part, it really does taste sweet.

So I'm feeling like I have had a win. My son feeling kind is one of those 'yep, you're doing OK' moments for me. I'm feeling overwhelming gratitude for everyone who helps our kids feel kind, too.

So, to all of the people who treat children with respect and kindness and don't expect things from them and instead just say 'Go for gold, you super little human!', thank you. Thank you for teaching kindness.

In a world where people are shooting up healthcare centres and concert halls, it's easy to feel overwhelmed by horribleness. It's easy to say 'What hope is there for a better whatever?'

I think there is hope. (And to be fair, if there isn't, that's even more reason to be kind, but I digress.) There's hope in kids feeling kind and being kind. And then, because someone made them feel special and loved and safe, they do the same for another. Little acts of kindness spreading like Marmite on dimpled cheeks and baby teeth.

THIS ISN'T INDULGENT

My nanna was a smart woman. She raised seven children. And had 18 (or probably more — it's hard to keep up) grandchildren.

I adored her.

She died before she could meet my children, which is heartbreaking in its own quiet way, but sadly not an unusual story for many of us. But her voice is often in my head when I feel challenged in parenting. I wish I'd spoken to her more about what it means to be a mother. When she died, I was footloose and fancy-free. I hoped we would one day have children, but to bring it up felt like tempting fate.

If I could turn back the clock I would have sat at her feet with a notebook. But as it stands, I have only the one bit of advice she gave my sister near the birth of her first child.

My nanna said: always go to a crying baby. You can't ever give too many cuddles. You can't spoil a baby.

I have inherited my grandmother's obsession with babies. I absolutely adore them. So that bit of advice rang true well before I had my own little one. But now, more than ever, it has guided me. And while I'm not one to buy into parenting philosophies, if I had one it would be something like this:

You're not being indulgent when you support your children through tough times.

You're not coddling them by being there for them when they need you.

You're not spoiling them by listening to them when they communicate with you the only way they know how.

It's such a tired old refrain that *parents these days* are too soft.

As if you need to be hard to raise children. To be unfeeling and cold to turn them out right. As if they're not children but dogs that need training so they don't chew your slippers or pee on the rug.

Children, even babies, need tough love, they say. They're manipulative, apparently. There's so much emphasis on discipline and the punishment of children, so little room for them to be human, let alone celebrated for being delightful.

It's not 'Maybe they're having a bad day, or maybe they're tired or overwhelmed', it's 'They need to be controlled, the parents need to rein them in, shut them up, they're "feral".'

Sometimes it's hard to tell whether these serial whiners are talking about children or animals. And there's the problem: of course you're never going to get that children are complex and just roll with it if a child's presence is confronting for you, if you don't even see them as human . . .

We have all seen or heard the rants about how *children these days* are running wild. There's no discipline. It's *easy* to get them to sleep at night, just turn off the light, shut the door, leave them. If they cry, they'll eventually stop.

To do any different is to 'overthink' parenting.

As if parenting is a thing that you should just not invest too much thought or time in. As if it's not your life's work but some kind of side hobby that requires little brain power.

These comments all suggest the same thing: by doing anything other than enforcing rules by ignoring children or by churning out seen-and-never-heard (actually, they would rather not even see them) little adults, you're being indulgent, you're coddling, you're spoiling.

And the by-product is that the kids are in charge, because Lord knows we have all heard or seen the 'You're the adult!' lecture, haven't we?

What these parenting legends (in their own lunchtimes)

don't realise in their race to their soapbox is that, actually, many of us are choosing to parent this way *for a reason*.

We are teaching lessons every time we make the choices we do — the choices they have decided are indulgent.

When my son cries out for me in the night and I go to him, and he is hot and sweaty, and his little heart is beating fast — when I go to him I am teaching him that he can always call on me, that I will always be there for him. If someone hurts him, he can tell me. If someone makes him feel unsafe, he knows he needs to call me. If he's scared, I'm here. Into his adult years I want him to know that unconditionally *I will be there*.

When I tell him Mama is here, and he takes my hand and puts it to his chest and I feel his heart beat slow and his chest begins to rise and fall with deep sleep, I am proud. I'm proud that I've taught him to seek help when he needs it, and to communicate that with the people around him who can help him.

If, growing up, he ever feels lost or hopeless, unstable or in pain, I hope I am teaching him that he can tell me and, no matter what, I'll help him in whatever way I can to get back on track.

When he breaks something precious and I tell him off, and he cries and cries and I pull him onto my lap and we cuddle, and I kiss his tears and we talk about feelings, I'm not coddling him. I'm teaching him that he must be careful with precious things, but he will always be precious. And we can get upset with each other, but it never changes how much we love each other. I know that it takes him time to really understand what he's done. That he won't get comfort if he's hurt is not the lesson I want to teach.

If, growing up, he is told boys don't cry, or that he has to be a man, or any of that toxic masculine bullshit, or that the way we teach each other to treat precious things gently is to hurt each other, I hope he will say 'No, that's not what I was taught.'

And when I don't feel like the adult and I lose my cool, or I stuff up, or I cry, and I say to him 'I'm sorry, Mama is tired' or 'Mama didn't mean to do that, I'm sorry', I am teaching him that I'm human, too, and I'm doing the best I can for this family, because we all love each other even when we aren't our best selves.

If, growing up, he falls short of his ideals, or he doesn't meet the expectations he has set for himself, I hope I have taught him that it's not the end of the world. That there's always tomorrow and that it takes more than a bad day to make a bad life.

I am teaching him to respect himself — that he is deserving of being treated fairly by others, including (in fact, especially) by his parents. I hope I'm teaching him to respect me and his father because we're human. We stuff up, but we try really hard not to.

I am teaching him honesty: that he doesn't need to hide his faults, or lie when something doesn't work out as he wanted it to.

I hope I'm teaching him that our love for him doesn't hinge on his ability to keep his shit together every second of every day.

And yes, he is three right now. But we've been doing this, the best that we can, since he was six pounds, seven ounces. And that started with doing the things that so upset the anti-coddle brigade.

Babies cry to communicate their needs in the only way they know how. I will not punish my child for asking me to meet his needs.

It's not indulgent to respond in the way we do. It's a choice. A choice to teach.

And a choice to follow in the footsteps of others who we trust. Thanks, Nanny.

HOW TO GET YOUR BABY OUT OF A SWADDLE

eeee

Hi! Is your baby incapable of going to sleep and staying asleep unless they're swaddled? Well, you've come to the right place! I'm here to teach you how to get your baby out of a swaddle in 50 easy steps!

Step 1. Loudly say to your significant other 'I think it's time for Baby to sleep without the swaddle'.

Step 2. Remove swaddle.

Step 3. Spend an hour and a half trying to hold down Baby's flailing arms as you try unsuccessfully to rock them to sleep.

Step 4. Sing them a lullaby.

Step 5. Slowly become aware that you're singing very loudly and aggressively as you lose your will to live.

Step 6. Give up. Put Baby back in swaddle.

Step 7. Forget pain of trying to get Baby to sleep without swaddle and again declare it is time to get Baby out of swaddle.

Step 8. Remove swaddle.

Step 9. Question how it is even remotely possible that Baby was comatose and yet is now wide awake and screaming because you laid them in their cot when they were not swaddled.

Step 10. Try to pat and shush Baby to sleep. Get partner to take over. Hear Baby screaming on monitor as partner tries to get Baby to sleep. Turn off monitor.

Step 11. Partner says they got Baby to sleep.

Step 12. Check on Baby and find them swaddled.

Step 13. Pour wine.

Step 14. Look at old photos from when you were thin and had money and didn't have children. Cry.

Step 15. Baby goes to sleep! You've done it!

Step 16. That wasn't too hard. Reward yourself by pouring a glass of wine.

Step 17. Baby woke because you were smug. Too bad. No wine for you.

Step 18. Imagine your child's future life-partner having to swaddle them before they go to sleep. Eat two litres of ice cream directly from the container.

Step 19. Google 'adult swaddles'.

Step 20. Look up on the WINZ website to see whether your child can get a home-based carer to handle their swaddling needs when they're an adult.

Step 21. Do nothing for two weeks.

Step 22. Tell your partner again Baby needs to sleep without a swaddle.

Step 23. When partner says to just leave them in the swaddle, consider divorcing them.

Step 24. You would have weekends to yourself if you were divorced. You'd miss your partner, sure, but it would solve the swaddling situation for at least a week at a time.

Step 25. Eat cold baked beans out of the can.

Step 26. Look at yourself, you're a disgrace! Put down those beans! You can do this! You can get Baby out of the swaddle!

Step 27. New resolve to get Baby out of swaddle. Rock Baby to sleep for 55 minutes.

Step 28. Tell partner he has to get Baby to sleep without the swaddle or you're going to jump off the balcony.

Step 29. Yell 'YOU CALM DOWN!' at your partner.

Step 30. Agree to address the swaddle issue when you get more sleep, even though the swaddle is waking your baby up at night, preventing you from getting more sleep.

Step 31. Get drunk and furiously yell at your computer screen while reading a blog post that says: 'If you really loved your child you would never have swaddled them in the first place.'

Step 32. Eat your weight in cookie dough.

Step 33. Give up. Do nothing for one month.

Step 34. Order eight different swaddles online that claim to be 'in-between swaddles'. Use none of them.

Step 35. Try to get Baby to sleep without swaddle. Give up after 15 minutes. Do nothing for one week.

Step 36. Decide Baby can just stay in swaddle.

Step 37. On 27th wake-up of the night, decide Baby cannot just stay in swaddle.

Step 38. Drunkenly call your friend. 'I'm the adult, right? Don't I get to decide?'

Step 39. After 45 minutes realise you didn't call your friend, you've just left a hysterical 45-minute message on your old employer's voicemail.

Step 40. Wonder if your baby will ever sleep through the night. Watch two episodes of *Fireman Sam* before you realise it's not *The Walking Dead*.

Step 41. Do nothing for three months.

Step 42. Loudly proclaim it's definitely time this time to get Baby out of a swaddle.

Step 43. Do nothing until it takes both you and your husband together to pull the zip up on the swaddle because your baby is almost one year old and is still being swaddled.

Step 44. Use duct tape to keep swaddle on.

Step 45. Drink heavily.

Step 46. Never sleep again.

Step 47. Baby breaks out of bottom of swaddle as their legs are too long.

Step 48. Make giant baby swaddle.

Step 49. Drink heavily.

Step 50. Begin again at Step 1.

WHY?

I have a constant (relentless) stream of commentary in my life from my exuberant two-year-old. We have recently hit the *why?* stage, which other parents had told (warned) me about.

My day usually starts with me trying very hard to respectfully and earnestly answer his questions in a patient and kind way befitting the kind of parent I like to imagine I am before reality smacks me in the face.

For example:

The toddler picks up the back of an earring: 'Whas that?'

Me: 'It's the back of an earring.'

'Whas that?'

'It holds the earring in your ear so the earring doesn't fall out of your ear.'

'Why?'

'Why do you not want an earring to fall out? Because you'd lose it.'

'No WHY?'

'Why would you wear an earring? Because earrings look nice.'

'Why?'

'Because they can be shiny or pretty or have colours. You like your shoes because they look cool. Mama likes her earrings because they look cool.'

'WHY?'

By the end of the day, the conversation is:

'Whas that?'

'I dunno, Eddie, it's a thing'

'Why?'

'It just is.'

Sometimes I end up having an existential crisis trying to work out how to answer him.

'Whas that?'

'A razor'

'What you doing?'

'Shaving my legs.'

'Why?'

'Because . . . I . . .ummm I don't like them hairy.'

'Why?'

'I umm . . . well . . . patriarchal standards of beauty dictate . . . ummm, probably subconscious societal pressures . . . I am . . . Mummy is a feminist but . . . there's . . . well . . .'

'Whas that?' *points to piece of fluff on the ground*

❂

'What choo doing dear Mama?' is heard around 67,000 times a day in my whare. I have started to provide a gratingly chipper commentary to attempt to pre-empt his interrogation:

'Mama is making a coffee.'

'Mama is soaking onesies after a poo explosion!'

'Mama is rocking and shushing and singing to the baby.'

'Mama is trying to get you to eat just one thing that isn't a biscuit.'

'Mama is losing her will to live.'

'Mama is imagining Jason Momoa naked changing the sheets on the bed.' (I'm too tired to even *imagine* anything more than that, and frankly not having to change the sheets is quite a turn-on in itself.)

Even though I'm providing constant updates, I still get WHAS THAT? WHAT CHOO DOING? WHY?

❂

And don't toddlers just have a wonderful way of expressing themselves in public when they practise their language skills? A while back I changed his nappy in the back of the car because he refuses to go into a public toilet without freaking out. The next day I told him we would need to do a nappy change and he yelled in the middle of the Warehouse: PLEASE DON PUT ME INNA BOOT DEAR MAMA I SORRY!

All of these alarmed shoppers stared at me. I tried to explain but it just came out as 'I don't . . . I mean, I put him in the boot once . . . but I was . . . He wasn't *in* the boot . . .'

Last week, his father yelled from the shower that the water had gone cold. I couldn't hear him over the sound of the shower, so he yelled to Eddie: 'Tell Mama the shower is cold!'

Eddie has decided to inform every single person we have met since that day: 'My deddy did yell at my dear mama and he did yell vewy loud at her. Den he did yell at Eddie vewy loud and he did yell at us a lot.'

We tried to explain there is 'bad yelling', which is angry, and 'raised voices because you can't hear because it's noisy, like when someone is in the shower'. That of course turned into telling strangers: 'My deddy said Eddie not say he yelling but he done yell.'

Thanks, kid.

✪

So I figure I'm just going to be more like my kid and just start asking WHY WHY WHY all the time. I thought I'd start with a list (because everyone likes lists, right?). Here are the Questions that are Impossible to Answer, Mama Edition:

* Why do public toilets with change tables have hand-dryers in them? They may as well have an actual fire in there. Kids would be less terrified.
* How is it that babies know when you pour a glass of wine?

You can time it perfectly with feeds, but as soon as the parent juice (oh dear God, that sounds revolting but I'm going to keep it) hits the glass they're like 'You rang?' Except instead of saying that they just scream as if they're being tortured.

* Would you get jail time if you hit your partner with a shovel for saying 'Baby slept well last night' in the morning when you woke up 800 times? Or would the judge see that as justifiable?

* Is there a line you can cross with food bribery? The other day I told my son I would buy him a lawnmower if he had one more bite of his toast. I've since discovered that lawnmowers are $800.

* Are people who buy toddlers Dora the Explorer sticker sets that have 10,000 stickers in them actually the Antichrist? Rhetorical question obviously — they are.

* Where are the pegs?

* How do kids have a shedload of toys and yet they have a meltdown if you chuck out the empty tissue box because that's their 'favroit waaaan'. How do they notice that you threw it away? Or is that just my children? Please say it's not just my children . . .

Finally: do you think they time their best lines for maximum impact? The other night I was so tired, almost to the point of tears, and the toddler climbed on my lap and said 'Fank you dear Mama for keep Eddie safe and love Eddie.'

I mean, *heart melt*.

I will buy you a lawnmower, my love. And replace the tissue box. And I promise I'll never put you in the boot again.

HOW NOT TO BE A JERK

Breastfeeding my fat little Ham, a woman leans over and says, 'He looks far too big for you to still be breastfeeding!'

Struggling to clip up my bra as he wiggles and jiggles, I hear, 'How old is he? You don't need to breastfeed past six weeks.'

My chubby and happy baby cries out in anger over a dropped toy: 'Are you breastfeeding? He's probably hungry, poor thing! He needs a bottle!'

'A little boy? You probably need to use formula, too, because boys need more milk than girls!'

'My baby slept through the night from birth — but that's because I didn't breastfeed.'

'It's a shame your husband can't help you with anything because you choose to breastfeed — my husband was really hands-on because we formula-fed. It's important for the baby to have both parents.'

'How long are you going to breastfeed for?'

'Don't you think it's time to stop?'

'When are you going to wean?'

'Is he getting enough milk?'

'You should give him a bottle top-up. That's what formula is for!'

'Do you still feed overnight?'

'I choose sleep, that's why I don't breastfeed. I don't know why you bother!'

'How many feeds is he having?'

'What are you going to do when you go back to work?'

HOW ABOUT YOU GET OFF MY TITS?

They're mine. Not yours. I'm not asking you to breastfeed my child, so why do you care about what I'm doing? Do I ask what you're doing with your nipples? No, I don't. So why ask me? All the bloody time. Do you want daily updates? What answer should I give to make you back off?

It shouldn't matter to anyone how people are feeding their kids. I can't believe we are still having this inane debate. But here we are. I wasn't even going to write about this, but another incredulous 'Are you still breastfeeding?!?' comment has tipped me over the edge.

Yes, if you must know, I am *still* breastfeeding my infant baby tiny child who is only nine months old. Because he is a baby. Babies need fluid. This is how the world works. Saying 'Are you still breastfeeding?' is the weirdest, dumbest question ever — my tit isn't in his mouth for kicks. You can see with your own eyes that I am. And if I'm not breastfeeding right then and there and I'm asked, what's the point of the question? What does it matter? If I asked everyone to tell me when you're meant to stop breastfeeding, everyone would give a different date — so what's the point in talking about it? How about since it's my body, I decide?

If you don't like people breastfeeding past a couple of weeks, that's fine. Here is what you should do about it: go outside, yell at a tree. Because nobody cares.

As long as I don't ask you to breastfeed my child, as long as I don't try to breastfeed *you* — you shouldn't be opening your mouth and saying anything about my tits to me. You shouldn't care. If for some reason you do — and I don't know why, but whatever — that's your weird deal. But you need to not say this to breastfeeding mums.

Likewise you need to STFU about formula-feeding. I've done both — expressed breast-milk and formula for my first and breast-milk direct and formula for my second. And I find the endless blog posts and coffee-group chatter about both desperately boring. Hell, this rant is boring! *But* the reason why we keep having this conversation is because people *keep being jerks*.

Of all the interesting things you can talk to mums about — child development, gummy smiles, novelty onesies, the rights of little people, how kids play, the funny ways they say words, what wine is on special at Pak'nSave, how to blow raspberries, little booties, paid parental leave, white noise apps, Kmart, fat cheeks, music babies love and how they dance, things that make them smile, types of coffee, poo, first words, hot dads, hot mums, fresh newborn baby smell, best playgrounds, least-annoying Disney songs, parenting wins, parenting fails, how to get them out of a damn swaddle, fluffy hair, yummy cuddles — all of those things, and all you can think to do is make a comment about whether the baby is bottle-fed or breastfed?

Try harder. Try instead:

What a beautiful baby.

OR

Here's some money.

OR

I bought shoes from a drug dealer once, I don't know what they were laced with, but I was tripping all day.

OK, I'm sorry about that one.

Mainly, though, people need to quit saying shit to mums they would never ever say to anyone else. Think: 1. Is it my business? 2. Do I need to know? 3. Will asking achieve anything at all?

Question why it bothers you, and question whether it *should* bother you — this applies to *everything* to do with parenting and unsolicited advice. Before you make a comment to someone about their, say, sleeping arrangements with their kids, think about what commenting on it is going to achieve. So you'd *never* have your kids in your bed. Cool, here's your medal. Now, is this mum or dad asking you to have their child in your bed? No? Are you wanting to sleep in their bed? No? So why are you upset? Why say anything?

Everyone is tired and muddling their way through — this is the default position of parents.

Just muddle through and don't get worked up about how anyone else is doing something.

Unless they're trying to breastfeed you. In which case — yeah, say something.

Otherwise, don't be a jerk.

THE SEA

Someone said to me 'You always find the joy', and I wish I could do that. And she looked like she was going to cry, and I very nearly cried at the time, and reflecting back on it I can't stop the tears.

I'm crying because I sincerely wish that were true. I'm sitting on the floor of the bathroom writing this. I am beyond exhausted. Today I really and truly feel like I have nothing more to give.

There were so many wake-ups last night I just stopped counting. I didn't sleep at all. There's nothing poetic or special or honourable in sleep deprivation. It's just awful.

I feel completely overwhelmed and numb. I am trying to stop the tears before my oldest wakes up so that I don't alarm him. The last thing he needs is to wake up to me being a mess.

The day lies ahead as if it's a churning sea. I don't know how I'm ever going to get through when I feel like I don't even have a life raft.

But then — I do know I've been here before.

I've run my fingers along the tiles as I cried.

And then Eddie has climbed onto my lap and kissed my cheeks and said 'You tired dear Mama? Is OK jus go sleep I watch baby Wonnie' and I've laughed. And laughing has made him laugh. An unsure chuckle at first and then a huge burst of giggles.

And I'll squeeze him tight and say, 'Do you know how much I love you?' And he'll say '24' because that's the biggest number he knows.

And then the baby will blow raspberries and we will laugh again.

I'll stand up. Wash my face. And we will have a good day.

I've been here before, and I'm sure you have, too. Maybe we do have a life raft and the sea only looks heavy and dark from here. Maybe when we get closer it's calmer. We will make it OK.

We will find the joy.

LET KIDS BE KIDS?

It seems that the phrase 'let kids be kids' is having a resurgence. Don't get me wrong — I'm into it. In fact, I say it a lot. And I believe it. But to me that slogan isn't just about the clothes they wear — or letting little boys wear tutus and nail polish and little girls play with trucks and have short hair.

What I want to talk about is what I call Normal Toddler Behaviour. Also known as Tantrums.

Here's my Let Kids Be Kids view:

Tantrums are normal and healthy and helpful. Don't get me wrong — they suck for parents. Like, really suck. My heart (and head, to be honest) hurts sometimes when I see my son struggling with his feelings and feeling overwhelmed. I want to put everything in order for him, help him contain all of the bubbling emotions, support him through the scary pressure he has welling up within him. That to me is my job as a parent — when he's having a hard time, I have to help him through it.

But the fact that he needs help? Normal. Completely normal. Toddlers are not adults with developed brains. There are people in their twenties, their thirties . . . hell, there are people at the end of their lives, at 80 and 90, who struggle to keep their emotions in check. We allow that (to an extent), so why do we insist (some parents with actual, brutal force) that children must keep themselves in control of their changing emotions and hormones at all times?

We so encourage learning — oh, you can count! Wonderful! Draw a house! Write your name! — but it seems learning how to *be* — how to manage your feelings, name them, work with them, adapt, change — is some kind of secret process that only happens by shutting the hell up in public and keeping away from any nearby adults.

How often have you had to rush away from a public place because you're getting glares because your toddler is going through Normal Toddler Feelings? How many times have you had to sit through lectures about how to 'control' your child? How to get them to bend to your will, obey you, be quiet — as if that's 'good behaviour', because they're not acting like, ummm, children.

So what would happen if everyone just accepted that children get overwhelmed sometimes and can't process things and get scared and stressed and their feelings explode a bit every now and then? How would the world change? For children? For their parents? For society as a whole?

What if we didn't have to bundle children into cars and race away from public places and make them *quiet* and make them smaller and make them take up less space because even if they're not having a terrible tantrum they *might* have a terrible tantrum?

At my son's birthday, one of his little besties became overwhelmed by everything and got very upset. Normal Toddler Behaviour. Her lovely parents cuddled her, talked to her, took her outside for some space, negotiated, helped her through this hard time she was having. At the time I'm sure it was overwhelming for them, but all I kept thinking about was what a wonderful little girl she is. She's clever and funny and sassy and adorable and spirited and happy! She has this incredible little magical grin. My son adores her. I adore her! Her parents adore her.

I also thought, thank God they're comfortable here and they don't feel like they have to go home. Because nobody at the party minded at all, because here, I'm saying it again: it's

Normal Toddler Behaviour. Normal. All toddlers do it. Every one. They're learning. Every day.

This wondrous little sprite has parents who are helping her learn. She's learning. They're learning. We are all in this together, making space so our kids can grow freely and *be kids*.

She quickly settled down in time to do a beautiful 'oh my goodness!' reaction to a visit from Elsa to the party — and I'm so glad she didn't miss that. She had a wonderful morning.

How many great little life moments do our kids and their parents miss out on because so many people won't let them be kids? Insist they're seen and not heard — and sometimes not even seen? That a child crying is just too much for us to handle in a public space?

Pffft. Let kids be kids. A tantrum is normal. That child is learning. The parents are learning. You can learn too — learn to make space for children and let them grow.

THOMAS THE COLONIALIST TANK ENGINE AND SODOR THE CAPITALIST NIGHTMARE

I hate *Thomas the Tank Engine*. I hate it. I think Thomas is a naïve, arrogant jerk who sacrifices other trains to further his career and suck up to the Fat Controller. Sodor is quite frankly a capitalist nightmare. Trains are sent to the scrapyard if they're not Useful. And we all know what that means — it means they're executed. They execute workers who don't work hard enough! Anyone who isn't Very Useful is goneburger.

There are no unions in Sodor, that's for sure. And that's not even the most messed-up thing about Sodor, either. Don't get me started on how lacking the show is on the representation of women. The women trains are actually girl carriages. You don't need to have a master's in gender studies to read between the lines on that one. Either they have no personality (Daisy) or they spend all their time giggling and chasing after Thomas and the other dude-bro engines nagging them (Annie and Clarabelle). I feel like there's a weird subtext about lady trains and that-time-of-the-month as well, but I'm very tired and certainly not very useful right now.

What about Hiro? Poor Hiro was taken as a slave. He dreams of his homeland. But when he's too old to work anymore, after a lifetime of service, do you think his 'owners' will let him go home? Hell, no! Coz this is Sodor and life on Sodor is an endless grind of working until you die. You're Useful or you create Confusion and Delay and you're dead. Hiro ends up wasting away in the damn forest! But this is a better fate than being slaughtered by Topham Industries AKA The Government.

Thomas finds him and, of course, dobs him in to 'help' him get back to his home. Thomas signed Hiro's death warrant and he didn't even realise because he can't see beyond his white privilege! He doesn't know that one day he won't be Useful anymore. And ain't nobody going to save him then.

I especially hate *Thomas the Tank Engine* because my son loves it. Somebody bought him one train and that was it. It's like an addiction. It's toddler crack. And he can't say 'Thomas the Tank Engine' he says 'Thomas the Asian', and when we are out *in public* he yells at me to get him an Asian. Or he yells, 'WE-AHS MY ASIAN MAMA' and I have to really loudly yell, 'I don't know where your ENGINE is. Maybe your ENGINE is in the car. No, I won't buy you another ENGINE.'

And someone, one day, will buy your child a Thomas train that won't fit on the tracks you have. And the tracks you have won't go with the other tracks someone else will buy you. And you will have eight different tracks that don't go together and you will need a second mortgage to actually build just one figure-eight track and have the trains to go with it.

And I think I'm just going to double-down on this rant . . .

I hate Jeff from The Wiggles. Screw you, Jeff. Why are you always sleeping? You don't do anything. Do you know how much I want to sleep, Jeff? But if I just go to sleep instead of looking after my kid I'll be reported to the authorities. Do your job, Jeff.

I also hate Elmo. My husband keeps telling me that Elmo is three and a half and I have unrealistic expectations about his behaviour. But fuck that. Elmo is an entitled little prick. And Abby — I hate Abby. Why do the adults on *Sesame Street* never stop Abby from doing her 'magic' when they know she will fuck it up? Why is there so little adult supervision on that street? They all pop in for a song, but then they just piss off after rattling off a few numbers or some dictionary definition. Maybe hang around and actually stop Abby. She's out of control. And stop whining, Big Bird. How old are you, anyway?

What is up with Mr Noodle? Just no. Why does an adult man need to be taught how to throw a ball? And why does he live in the closet of a three-and-a-half year-old's house?!

And it's not just TV. *flails* *Books!*

Maisy, you are illogical. Why would a mouse be friends with a chicken? Why is everyone always shaming Eddie for not fitting into places? He's a fucking elephant. What did you expect?

Rock on, Scuffy the Tugboat. Don't let the man bring you down. They might be telling you not to chase waterfalls and to please stick to the rivers and the lakes that you're used to, but that's because they're classist. You have just as much right to hang out with the barges as any other boat. Keep on keeping on, Scuffy.

And the worst: *Love You Forever*. Damn, woman! Leave your kid alone. Let him sleep! When he turned nine, you should have been assessing your health. It's just not good news when you're that fixated on your child not growing up. Getting on a bus at night and breaking into his house so you can sniff him when he's a grown-ass man? That's *not right*. And if you had to call him to tell him you're sick, you clearly don't have a great relationship — and that's probably because *you are breaking into his house at night and touching him while he sleeps*. And dude, I know your childhood was hard-core what with your mum creeping on you every night and not respecting your boundaries, but you need to break the cycle!

So I guess it's just *Jay's Jungle*, *Play School* and Margaret Mahy books in this house.

Jay, you're great. You just keep being a lovely, singing, handsome man. While I think it's mildly narcissistic that the island you live on is shaped like a J, and it's weird that your 'friend' is a talking lighthouse, I'm willing to let that slide because of your soft, sensuous singing voice. You keep being you, Jay.

CHOOSING

I'm often asked for parenting advice. Usually I respond with a kind of pained and awkward grunt. I'm not an expert on anything — but I am especially not an expert on parenting. I have no idea how to make a baby sleep. I don't know when you should introduce bottles. Making kids eat — it's a mystery to me. Dealing with tantrums? Maybe, I dunno, pretend it's someone else's child?

See? I'm no good with advice.

I think I am so wary of giving advice because I'm unsure a lot of the time. I never quite know if what I'm doing is *The Right Way to Parent*. I don't have a philosophy. I chop and change as my children change. Parenting reminds me of those theme-park rides where you have to stand on a wobbly board. The ground is always moving. I admire parents who are utterly sure of *how to do things*.

I am not one of those parents.

But . . . there is one particular thing I do which has worked for quite some time now. And it's been wonderful for me and my son. And I think it will be wonderful for my youngest son, too. And maybe it will be wonderful for you and your child.

OK, so, here it is — I'm not going to build it up:

I let my kids dress themselves.

I know, right? You're let down. That is not very exciting. But I tell you what — it has made a huge difference in our lives and it's bigger than it seems.

From when my son was very small but able to communicate, I let him pick what clothes he wanted to wear. When he could talk, I allowed him to pick clothes at the store.

Kids have so little control over their lives. This is one way I can give my son some control. I can say to him: I trust you to dress yourself. Giving him the chance to start his day by making some of his own choices has really helped us all have a less stressful (I'm not going to say stress-free — that would be a lie) morning.

Sometimes it's hard — early on I had to accept that some days he wants to wear that shoe on that foot but also he wants to wear one gumboot. And I've had to say OK. Fine.

Sometimes it's awkward — like when people say 'Is your son wearing a colander on his head?' or 'Is he wearing a pair of adult women's stockings over top of pyjama pants?' There was quite a bit of that at the start as he got excited about the endless possibilities (*I want to wear all of my socks!*) but for us, at least, the novelty wore off quickly . . .

Sometimes it's not as practical as it could be — like when it's cold and he insists on wearing shorts. (I work my way around this by saying it's a shorts day or it's a long pants day at the start.) But he also learned quickly that he doesn't like being cold, so now dresses appropriately.

Overall, though, it works. And the wonderful thing about it is that I'm getting to know him even more by how he expresses himself. I love seeing what he picks and doesn't pick. I love the outfits and his reasoning for them: 'Today is a red day' or 'I have to wear mine googles because I am an moon man.'

I am also teaching him that I want him to love what he loves. I want him to express himself, to find his way — and letting him choose the way he dresses is a way to encourage that.

I would not be able to handle someone picking my outfits and telling me what I can and can't wear. I have become a lot more particular about my aesthetic as I've aged. How I dress is how I show the world who I am. Hard edges so they know not to fuck with me, femme — but on my terms.

It's a journey of self-discovery and I think it's one that kids can really get on board with. If they're given the chance.

And this whole thing has taught me stuff, too — namely, not to think of my son as my mini-me. This created-in-my-image little person.

He's his own person.

The fact that he loves things I'm not into — princesses, pink, frills and softness — has reminded me I don't own him. He's not mine.

It's hard sometimes to remember he's a little individual with individual needs and he deserves autonomy.

Even at three?

Especially at three.

Seeing my son dressed in a tutu with three t-shirts on, a cape and a swimming cap is the perfect reminder to me that he needs to be treated as his own person.

The parenting advice, the experts, Those Who Know It All, be damned. They don't know my kid. But I do, and he knows himself.

That's all I need to know. I have to parent my child the way *he* needs to be parented. Not the way it should or shouldn't be done according to someone who doesn't know him.

THREENAGER

ℓℓℓℓ

At the park today it again dawned on me that I really need to
work out how to, ummm, _deal with_ my threenager's behaviour.
He's (in my opinion) a really well-behaved kid, so I don't often
have to imagine up punishments for dodgy deeds. But then,
I'm told I'm quite permissive. I don't think I am — I'm just of
the view that a lot of the things people freak out about are just
normal kid behaviour.

Being noisy is normal. I'm not going to tell him off for that.
I'm also unlikely to take him to a place where he has to be
silent. But then cathedral tours or funerals aren't on our to-do
list, so this doesn't impact us much.

Eventually, when he's at an age where he understands what
'inside voice' means, it won't be an issue. So really, I don't see
the point in wrapping myself in knots trying to get him to _be quiet_.
Especially when I end up yelling and he's yelling — I mean, now
there's two people making too much noise. And I find adults
yelling far more stressful to listen to than kids yelling.

Likewise with running. Sometimes the kid just needs to run.
So we go to the dog park or to the beach so he can run. There's
no point when he's in a running mood to suggest we go to high
tea or a movie. If the kid wants to run, I let him run. And I try
not to get annoyed at him when I've picked an activity that
doesn't suit the needs of his three-year-old brain and body at
that time.

I get it wrong at times (a lot of the time), of course — and
there are some times when we are somewhere where he just has
to deal with not getting his way. Like the supermarket. My way

of dealing with supermarket tantrums is to make my husband do all of the supermarket shopping.

See, as you can tell, I'm not only not an expert, I'm basically largely incompetent when it comes to this kind of stuff. Avoidance and the path of least resistance are my way of handling potential and actual meltdowns. If there's a public meltdown I'll usually just bundle him in the car and leave. I can't be bothered with an audience when I'm trying to work out how to parent.

I've never been able to understand when you're supposed to *know what to do*. I mean, do people read books? Is that how they know? Or do they just know?

I remember my son's first tantrum. I just stared at him — my jaw almost hit the floor. All I could think was: *What the hell is he doing?* Then: *Why is he so upset? What just happened? Why is he losing his shit over nothing?*

It was such a shock when the tantrums started. I asked a few friends what they did, and some had 12-step programmes and others just had wine. I read online a lot of things I *should* be doing that just didn't feel right. I mean, I'm not going to hit my kid full stop, but I'm especially not going to hit them when they're upset. So I kind of attempted this terrible Attempt Everything plan which really didn't work.

I would say: 'Umm, excuse me — that is definitely a time-out. Go to your room.' And then he'd say: 'OK.'

And he'd go to his room and play with his toys. And I'd be like: Awesome! This is great — I can read a magazine! I have clocked parenting.

And then he'd come upstairs and say 'That was a nice time-out', and I'd be like: *I am a great mother, I punished him and he doesn't even know he was being punished and I got to pick up a magazine and read the same sentence 15 times because I'm too tired to absorb it.*

But then one day I said, 'Go to your room. That's a time-out' and he said:

'NO.'

And I said: 'Well, you have to.'

And he said: 'But I dun wan to.'

And I said: 'That's kind of the point, Eddie. This is meant to be a punishment.'

And he said: 'I dun wanna punmishmen.'

And I thought it was so cute I said, 'Aww, have a hug instead,' and we read a story.

And I was again, like, *This is OK, right? This is distraction! That's a good technique for dealing with behaviour I don't want, right?*

And I just went on my merry way and kept doing stuff like that, and then today at the park I said, 'It's time to go, Eddie. We need to get home.' And he said:

'NO.'

And so I said: 'Come on, Eddie — now.'

And then I waited five minutes while he ignored me.

Another mum looked at me and I felt like I had to say something, so I said, 'Don't make me say it again. Come now.'

I literally said it again as I said: 'Don't make me say it again.'

He ignored me.

'Don't make me come in there,' I said as I went in there.

He ignored me.

I felt like other mums were looking at me, when in all likelihood they were probably just thinking about whether it's socially acceptable to drink wine at a playground (that's what I was thinking, so maybe I'm projecting).

'I'm going to count to three, Eddie!' I said.

He ignored me.

'One.'

He ignored me.

'Two.'

He ignored me.

'I said "two", Eddie. Don't make me get to three.'

He ignored me.

'Two and a third, Eddie! That's a fraction. That means one out of three, Eddie.'

He ignored me.

'Two and a half! Two halves make a whole!'

I was getting quite manic now.

He ignored me.

'Two and like four-fifths, Eddie. I will say three next, OK?'

I was starting to sound like the crazy person I am.

He ignored me.

'Three!'

He ignored me.

Fuck.

I didn't know what I was meant to do at three! I can't believe I'd started this when I had no idea what was going to happen at three. I'd seen other parents count and it had worked, so I figured it would work for me. Isn't there meant to be some magical thing that happens at three? I have to do something now or else I'll never be able to use the 1-2-3 trick again! But then it's a pretty fucking useless trick if it doesn't work, right? Oh God, did anyone hear me say three? Am I meant to be doing something? Is he too young for 1-2-3? Is that why it didn't work? Is he too old for it? Maybe I should just start counting again? Maybe it's five? Maybe three is not enough time to get him to do what I want him to do? Maybe it's the 1-2-3-4-5 trick and not the 1-2-3 trick. Three counts isn't that long, am I being unfair on him? No! I have been telling him we have to go now for half an hour. I am the parent! I don't ask him, I tell him. But then . . . he was busy doing something, and maybe we don't have to leave immediately. Jeez, if we didn't have to leave straight away why did I start this 1-2-3 shit? Can I use it now when I'm in a situation where we actually *do* need to leave immediately?

CAN I DRINK WINE IN A PLAYGROUND AT 11 A.M.?

As I had an existential crisis about how to handle my kid, I was suddenly snapped back to reality by a tug on my jersey. It was Eddie.

'Can we go now? I hungry Mama.'

JUST YOU WAIT

~

Like a Greek chorus, all you seem to hear when you're pregnant and when you have young children is 'Just you wait!' or 'You'll see!'

As you mop your brow struggling with a toddler who wants to climb onto (or, hell, into) your 36.5-week swollen belly, you're told 'Think it's tough now? Wait until the baby is here!'

As you voice your exhaustion, with deep bags under your eyes as your oldest tears around the room and your baby wails in your arms, you're told 'Wait until the wee one is walking! Then you'll be busy!'

As you rock your baby in the front-pack and push your buggy with a protesting two-year-old raging inside it, inevitably someone will feel the need to say 'You think this is hard? Wait until they both want to go into the buggy!'

I don't know what's behind this incessant urge to say 'It's going to get worse.' or 'You think babies are hard? Wait until you have toddlers!' or 'You think toddlers are hard? Wait until you have a two-year-old!' or 'You think this age is hard! Try a threenager!' or 'Preschool is easy, wait until they're at school!' Then there are the ones with teenagers who insist that babies are a breeze compared to their kids.

By the time this book is published I will have a two-year-old and a four-year-old. It will be easier than it is now. It will still be hard. Definitely. I will still struggle and have hard days. That is parenting. The best things in life are often the hardest.

But I'll definitely be getting more sleep than I am now. And I won't be so tied to my house. I'll be able to go to a movie every now and then. My kids will be old enough to both stay overnight with family. I'll be able to get a babysitter and not feel guilty or feel like I need to check in all night. I'll be able to drink a coffee on a bench with friends while my kids play at the playground.

Every month that goes by I'm struck by the little things that change but make such a huge difference. Only a few months ago I cried regularly through the torture of sleep deprivation. I dreaded the evenings: the endless wake-ups until I finally fell into bed, only to be launched awake again to the sound of screaming. Now, I'm starting to claim my evenings again. I can see myself being able to start dance classes again. I can see myself taking shaky first steps into the outside world again on my own with my babies asleep in their rooms.

Actually asleep.

My body feels like my own again after breastfeeding for more than a year. I felt privileged to have been able to feed my second baby; it's something I wasn't able to do very well at all with my first.

But I don't miss breastfeeding. And I love the freedom I am starting to get back.

The Just You Wait chorus is wrong.

Just you wait, because you're going to get a bit more of yourself back soon. Just you wait until you meet the day without the throb of broken sleep in your brain. Just you wait — the fog of sleep deprivation will be lifted soon. Just you wait — you'll feel more confident and more assured.

Your baby will grow in front of your eyes and it won't be the curse they claim it to be. You'll look at your children and your heart will burst.

You made them. You nursed them. You nurtured them. They thrive because of you.

You did this.

And they'll keep growing and some things will be so much easier. Some things won't be easier, but I promise they'll be different.

And sometimes, when you're looking down the barrel of a new day with no sleep, that's what you need to hang onto.

Different is coming.

Easier is coming.

There is joy now, there will be joy soon, and there will be joy well into your future. Being a parent doesn't begin or end at any stage. There's wonder and love and happiness at all ages.

Just you wait.

ALWAYS OUR BABIES

The Ham was so sick today. His fat little cheeks were red and hot. His eyelashes wet and his forehead clammy. He pressed himself against me as close as he could get.

As I sipped a cuppa I didn't notice straight away that he'd fallen asleep on me.

For the last few months I have watched him take unsure steps and I have watched him run well before he could walk. I've watched him learn how to ride his little trike and hold a spoon. I thought it was adorable. Watching him learn how to open the toilet door was not so adorable.

Still, many times in the last few months I have thought — wow, he's really a toddler now.

Today I am reminded that he's still my baby.

I've been transported to those early days when he was so new to me and the world. When we were getting to know each other in the safe confines of our little home.

Those early days were so heartbreakingly beautiful. There's something so wondrous about the way that time slows so in those first heady days of mothering. My memories of those days are bathed in a soft light.

I blocked out the world in those early days. We cocooned ourselves, us four.

I don't want to go back to that time because I'm happy where we are. But thinking about those days makes me feel safe.

As Ham snuggles into me, softly snoring, I can't help but think about safe places.

I am a safe place to my children. I often see my oldest

son crumple in my presence after a long day at kindy or out with friends. It used to frustrate me — why did he save his grumpiness for me? And then I realised that it was with me that he felt safe to just let it all out. Just as I paint on a smile in social occasions and then crumple into my husband and cry, they too know that they don't have to be anything or anyone else for me.

There's no greater privilege than to be the safe place for someone. For our children and our partners.

The one we need when we are sick. When we are weary. When we just need help to feel better.

Those early days prepare you. Get ready, they say. You're a home now. You're a home to your babies forever.

Sometimes I try to look to the future and I imagine myself and my husband old and grey. Laughter lines and tired eyes.

And two little boys have grown.

But they still come home to us when they need us.

We will always be a home to our babies.

ME TIME

On my first day away from both kids, in another city, I feel utter freedom. My children and family are a golden thread stitching my life together. To be away from them isn't to unpick that thread, rather to take a moment to enjoy the delicately woven fabric of my new life.

It saddens me to see passive-aggressive comments all over the net shaming mums for taking time away from their kids. The martyrdom of motherhood doesn't help anyone. Taking time out, if it's at all possible, is a privilege and in my opinion something you *should* do as a mum.

Absence makes the heart grow fonder and blah blah blah, but also *freedom is sweet!*

My trip away is for 'work' — a few days away for writing. But my gosh, it tastes good. I have not been apart from my children in almost two years.

Even the trip through the airport was delicious. Did you know that without children you can get your boarding pass and dump your bag within *minutes*? I bought a coffee. And I drank it while it was hot.

My stroll to my gate was a damn stroll! No rushing, no sweating.

People without children have well and truly lost the right to complain about travelling.

It was relaxing. Because it was just me, alone. Nobody hanging onto me. No 'Mum, I'm hungry!' No agitated rushing from my husband. No baby pooping himself immediately before take-off. No stressed-out shushing of a screaming child.

I bought a magazine for the flight. And I read it. I say this not to make you hate me. If you're reading this with a baby literally attached to your body, I apologise. I say it to tell you that the simple act of taking time out, even if you don't do *anything*, is sacred and fortifying.

Even if you don't go away for a weekend, or fly anywhere (mine was a domestic flight — 45 minutes to freedom). If it's at all possible — run. Run from your children. For an hour, a day, a weekend, a week. Race into that ridiculous 'you-time' illusion that's only a reality if your children are *not near you*.

To have time that belongs only to you allows you to rebuild. It's beautiful and it's needed.

Trust me. If you can — take it. Take time and eat it up and don't share it with anyone.

DISGUSTING FOOD

The other day I made my son a luncheon sandwich. Instead of bread, though, I used luncheon. So it was basically three pieces of luncheon together. He declared it the best thing he's ever eaten and said 'I only wan dat for my life ever.'

And I was, like, of course you do. Of course you want to eat only gross food that has very little (if any) nutritional value.

What is it with kids and their love of fake meat? Luncheon and cheerios and chicken nuggets are a staple of their diet. They're my guaranteed go-to foods.

It's almost impossible to get him to eat, but he will always eat luncheon. Cheerios and chicken nuggets are a solid back-up plan.

My grand plans about no processed food disappeared out of the window as the lovingly prepared unprocessed food basically went out of the window, too.

He knows what he likes. And what he likes is cheese, but not the good kind. Just the plastic-wrapped and plastic-tasting type. I guess blandness is something he's into when it comes to eating.

But I will give him the food that gets eaten. I will keep trying (of course) to provide more nourishing fare, but I am of the view that he will grow out of this. I mean, adults don't eat luncheon.

Once my son earnestly told me that he was going to be a vegetarian. I explained to him that chicken nuggets are made from chicken. If he wanted to be a vegetarian I'd support him, but it would impact him, given his favourite foods.

He was scandalised. I don't know where he thought chicken nuggets came from (the clue is in the name, my darling) but he was not happy about this new discovery. To soften the blow I explained to him that the chicken nuggets he ate were cheap and pre-frozen so probably didn't have that much actual chicken in them.

That didn't help.

He looked at me with his big blue eyes and said 'What an bout luncheoned?'

Sorry, sweetheart — luncheon is basically, like, heaps of animals. I don't even know what kind, to be honest.

Surprisingly, he wasn't alarmed by this, but still was quite set on being a vegetarian.

But one that ate luncheon.

And chicken nuggets.

And cheerios.

Bless.

I decided to eat a piece of luncheon the other day. I thought maybe it would bring me to a time in my childhood when I adored it. That maybe I'd understand why he thought it was the Best Food Ever.

It was disgusting.

Adults don't eat luncheon.

EDDIE'S STORY

My son said to me once, 'Tell me the story of when I was sick.' And I looked at his little moon face, looking up at me expectantly, and I knew I couldn't just yet. He was snuggled up on me with his little hands tucked into the neck of my jumper, his long legs a little pretzel in my lap.

He has a favourite game where he gets a long ribbon or scarf or a pair of my stockings stolen from the clothes horse and ties it to me. I pretend I don't notice him doing it so that I can feign surprise when he says: 'YOU ARE MINE NOW! WE ATTACHED!'

He doesn't know I'm his always. We will always be attached. He doesn't need to trap me, he has my heart always. He did from the first time I heard the little gallops of his heartbeat as I lay on the hard bed in my midwife's office.

'I think it's a boy,' she said.

We knew then, too. We knew our little boy before we met him because we had dreamed of him for so long.

So I will tell him his story here. Ready for when he's too big to fit in my lap and he wants to hear about the little boy who made it.

Once upon a time I was pregnant.

I was pregnant just like every other pregnant person and I had the same thoughts and the same feelings and the same wishes as they did.

In the wee small hours, before I ever knew how fraught those hours could be, I'd lie in bed and put my hand on my belly and I'd imagine I was touching my baby's face.

I imagined him constantly. I imagined blue eyes and blond

hair, and brown eyes and brown hair. I imagined a baby without even a bit of hair. I imagined his toes and his fingers, and I imagined his laugh. I imagined rocking him and singing to him. I imagined our future together. I imagined swings at the park and first days of school, and him one day bringing home someone he loves and saying to them 'This is my mum.' I imagined cuddles and I imagined tears (not many, though). I imagined jobs he might have and I imagined values we would instil in him. I imagined the stories we would tell him and the stories he'd tell us.

I never imagined he would be sick.

When he was born they took him away and they said he needed help to breathe. It's such a gentle way of saying 'your baby can't breathe'.

He was fixed up quickly and handed to my husband and we barely thought of that little moment when we had all held our breath with him. He could breathe. He did breathe. All was right in the world with our little baby.

And then people would say 'Does he always make those noises?' and 'Does he have a cold?' and 'Gosh! He's a loud snorer!'

And we kept going to the doctor and they kept saying 'It's stridor. It's fine.' There were comments about how *lots* of babies have stridor and we just said OK, *lots is lots.*

And we got used to the dragging sound and even made jokes about how he was a zombie baby.

And I don't know when exactly something changed, but we decided no, I don't think this is a *lots*-of-babies thing. I think our baby can't breathe.

And we said it out loud to the people who kept saying 'No, it's stridor', and eventually someone said to us, 'No, you're right. Your baby can't breathe.'

We learned everything happens quickly when you have a

baby who can't breathe. But it also happens slowly.

We were told he would have surgery and they used words with lots of syllables and we were scared and we looked up the name of the condition and the name of the surgery and the names of the bits that would be worked on and it scared us.

We were very brave, I think. Until we weren't.

On the day of his first surgery when he was still our tiny little baby who had just been born, we carried him into the room before the room where they take them away and operate. The room had a rainbow on the roof and I kept looking up at it, blinking away tears. I didn't want our little baby to know we were scared.

My husband took him in because I think they thought my son's fragile, bird-like disposition was inherited from me. They were right.

A nurse sent me back to the children's ward to wait after I had kissed my son's forehead and said *I love you* with the most conviction I've ever felt in my life.

And I walked the path home to the place that had become our home — the children's ward. And I thought — it would be useful if I had a religion right now.

But I don't have a religion. And I thought about praying one by one to all of the gods that other people believe in, and I thought they might take pity on this mum who couldn't feel the ground beneath her feet. I thought they might look at my son's tiny body and say — we need this one.

And then I thought, we don't get to make bargains. And other mothers have stood where I am now and their prayers haven't been answered, even as they loved their little babies as fiercely as I love mine. And all little babies with tiny bodies are needed. Every single one.

So I closed my eyes and I said to nobody and everyone: *Please.*

Just please. Please let me hold my baby again and let him smile that beautiful smile for me.

No bargains, no promises, no deals or compromises.

Just please.

✪

They told us he would go straight into the intensive care unit after his surgery. He would travel there on a gurney with one of us. I was on the bed faster than an Olympic hurdler and a sheet was draped over me, my chest bare for him.

He was placed on me and I was scared the ice in my blood from my fear would chill his tiny body. He had a breathing tube in, and when I try to think of how he looked my mind says no. It's like a little lady at an art gallery gently steering you away from a closed exhibit. *Move along now, dear. Nothing to see here.*

I remember being so scared to hold him, yet so desperate to hold him.

I remember the kindness of nurses.

I remember the kindness of doctors.

I remember the kindness on the faces of people going through a greater hell than I was.

There's so much sadness in the intensive care unit. And so much beauty, too. And we made it out, so reflecting back is different for us, too. But I will never forget the devastation that felt like it was dripping from the walls there.

And the love — so much love.

A family beside us sang to their loved one and farewelled them on to their next journey and we all cried for each other. Their waiata rose up and filled the room and I rocked my baby and tears fell and I watched his heart monitor and with every beat I said:

Thank you
Thank you

Thank you.

My mother-in-law, an absolute angel of a woman and a rock to us all, told my husband and me to take a break. Neither of us wanted to leave Eddie's side, but we knew he was safe with his beloved nanna while we ate dinner. She laid a hand on his forehead and I felt like I could feel and see the love between them.

We walked away, shoulders hunched, clutching hands just a little too tightly, eyes darting around as we entered back into Real Life.

The unit feels like a horrible dream, and it was jarring to walk into the bustle of the main hospital. We slumped into a couch and just looked at each other, but it was too much to say what we were thinking.

Relief, guilt, fear, worry . . .

✪

We had been told the test would be when his breathing tube was removed. If he coped on his own, we would be moved to the ward. The doctors seemed confident, but I saw them exchange glances, and a nurse put a loving but firm hand on my shoulder and gently pulled me away from the bed so there was room for them to work if they needed to.

The tube was removed and . . .

And . . .

He coughed violently.

Spluttered.

His eyes searched for us.

He gasped.

He saw his father . . .

He smiled.

It was more than a smile.

It was the world opening up for all of us. A future. Hopes!

Dreams! A gracious plenty!

A joyous chorus rose up, delighted laughs were quickly settled — we were not in a unit known for laughs — and the nurses beamed at me. I thought the doctor might high-five someone but he just nodded and said 'That's what we like to see' and moved on to the next bed.

I don't believe in miracles. I believe in the skill of doctors and nurses and incredible people whose life's work it is to help and heal. Those who treated our son were living, breathing miracles.

I thought about their mothers. I thought about how I want to meet these women and say, 'Did you know your child has changed my world? Did you know you raised someone who gave us all life and then clocked out as if it was a normal work day?'

✪

After he'd been settled for some time, breathing on his own, we made the move to the ward — again, me on the gurney and my precious baby on my chest.

As we left the ICU, I again felt the love of those we left behind. They have stayed in my heart always. I think of them often. I think of everyone who ends up in that unit — floundering, terrified, strong, loved.

Some kuia had taken over the kitchen by the unit to ensure their whānau were fed to last their ordeal. They smiled at me as we left. Oh māmā, they said to me, a silent prayer for me, a stranger. Even in a time of great need there is so much solidarity in these wretched places.

We made our way into the ward and were positioned next to the nurses' station. Eddie's vital signs were on a machine by the window with the curtain pulled around it.

I lay next to him as he slept and listened to the laughter of the nurses and the beep, beep, beep of the machine.

I don't remember a great deal more of that visit. Just that our little boy got stronger. With every breath he took we could breathe, too.

Life felt closer. A curtain pulled back, a window open, we are nearly there. We can join the world.

✪

When we took him home, it felt like the first time. With as much care as we had taken when he was first born, my husband put him in his carrier and then into the car. I sat in the back with him, unable to take my eyes from him.

A second chance.

Life keeps on. It's just like that. You go back to work. Your heart begins its normal beat again.

And then it doesn't.

A few weeks later we heard his breathing drag again and I felt like I was freefalling.

I had nightmares about children in wells and terrible fairy tales come true. I couldn't protect my baby from bears and wolves dressed as grandmothers and wickedness in the forest.

I threw myself into work while my husband cared for our baby at home. We listened constantly to his breathing and went back and forth to appointments at the hospital.

More surgery.

It was inevitable. But when?

And then it was decided for us. A simple cold was too much for our baby.

We had kept him isolated, but somehow he had caught a cold. I blamed myself. I was convinced I'd brought germs home from work even though my hands were raw from sanitiser.

We had an appointment at ENT and then suddenly they said 'He needs surgery right now.'

I called my sister to get her to pass on the news to the rest of the family.

'Oh hi . . . Sorry are you . . . at home? I . . . Eddie . . . he . . . well, he is going . . . to . . . have some surgery . . . Just a thing . . . with . . .'

My sister's voice broke through . . .

'Breathe', she said. 'Just breathe.'

I couldn't cope. I just couldn't. In my head I was screaming. I wanted to be the mother who held it all together. The mother who was brave. The mother who was sure. The mother who was calm. It's no use to anyone to be upset. The doctors know what they're doing. They can handle it. He's the one having surgery. Pull yourself together.

Pull. Yourself. Together.

'I'm fine. I'm good. I am. I will call. I'm OK. He will be fine. It's good. I'm OK.'

I quickly hung up and followed my husband. The ground beneath me felt unstable, so I asked him to keep carrying Eddie.

Outwardly we must have looked so calm. Only my husband's tense jaw gave away the fear I knew he felt.

We were in our own personal earthquake. Before we could find our feet and yell 'Are you OK?' our baby was in surgery.

We stood, struck dumb, outside the doors still swinging.

What had just happened?

Once again my husband's mother was a lifeline. Calm, unruffled, gentle.

I wanted to be a rock, but I wasn't. She was, though. We clung to her like children. With a cheeriness I actually believed, she told us everything would be fine.

I knew then that this is the type of mother I want to be as my children grow older. I want to be the cliché to my children: the rock, the monument to stability, the calm in the storm.

If this was our earthquake, she was our doorway. She sheltered us again as she had the first time Eddie had been operated on.

I utterly believed her when she said everything would be OK.

I trusted her as I have from the very first day I met her as a scattered, broken, barely-together teenager.

Again, Eddie pulled through and we made our way back to the ward again. Back to the familiar beeps and the nurses who always laugh and always deserve cake.

The surgeon saw us and said everything had gone well. They were pleased.

And then, as they outlined what they'd done, they said '. . . his next surgery' and it cut through the noise.

More? More surgery? How would we cope?

They explained that they hoped he wouldn't require more surgery, but it looked like he might. It was a waiting game. A game I've never wanted to play.

We returned to the world but it was a world of uncertainty. Of quickened pulse every time we heard his breathing drag. We kept him away from people who might not understand there's no such thing as 'just a little cold'.

We kept ourselves away, fragile but trying to just keep on.

And we did keep on. There was laughter and light and love, just as there is in the homes of healthy children. And we got used to the sounds of our son trying to breathe. And we had endoscopies and we were assured that he could breathe, it just sounded like he couldn't.

And we even went on holiday with a note from his care team that said 'He can breathe, this is a condition called X and this is just the way he sounds.'

And it kept on like that: 'He's fine, that's just the way he breathes', 'No, he doesn't have a cold, he's OK' and 'I promise you we know what we are doing, he can breathe, that's just what his breathing sounds like.'

And then more surgery.

And we felt like we were forever in the shadow of a beast. A looming terror. I was constantly terrified he would just stop breathing, even though we were assured he wouldn't. I was scared of coughs, and the sight of a runny nose made my bones ache. The hairs on the back of my neck would stand on end when someone would brush by me at work. I would imagine germs leaping onto me and then onto Eddie.

And we kept up with medications which were supposed to help but didn't.

And more endoscopies and then . . .

It's looking good.

They kept saying each day that went on would be better, and I didn't believe them in the way I'd believed my mother-in-law.

But they were right.

He slowly improved. Slowly and surely and beautifully.

Until we suddenly said one night: 'You can't hear him!'

Silence. He was breathing easily for the first time in two years.

And we realised we had been holding our breath for two years.

And we let out a sigh that carried the weight of our little world.

Safety for us, for our little boy who is our little world. Who gave us life and whose life was saved.

And every day that goes by I try to take a second — I take in his sparkling eyes, his soft golden hair, his rosy cheeks, his little teeth, his button nose, his big ears, his long legs, his skinny arms, his round little puku, the little creases when he smiles, his cheeky laugh, his gentle voice.

The way he says 'dear Mama' like a song.

I take it all in.

And I think of the monitor that measured his oxygen saturation levels and his heart rate and I think of the beeps and I hear them as if I am there and at every beep I say:

Thank you
Thank you
Thank you.

DEAR MAMA

Dear Mama I be taller than Deddy wan day.

You will be. You'll even be taller than Mama.

An Mama you want be able to pick me up cos I be too big!

Yes—

An Mama when I too big you will be smoll agen.

Yes, sometimes when you're very, very old you get smaller—

An when an when an when you are smoll I will carry you
dear Mama.

And just as I was getting teary about my gorgeous loving little
boy, he said:

YOU WILL POO IN YOUR NAPPY.

Excuse me — that's enough.

YOU WILL POO ON THE FLOOR AN YOU WILL SMELL.

Well . . . there's that moment gone . . .

YOU'LL MISS THOSE DAYS

Even as I rally against the nostalgia of others when they say 'You'll miss these days', I realise that I will. But there seems so few ways you can embrace this fact without feeling as if the soundtrack to your days is a ticking clock.

I know that as the days and weeks and months and years fly on, the harsh edges of these baby days are softened. I forget. Because of course we do. Why should we hold onto the way those baby days hurt? There's no need for memories of isolation or loneliness. No space to hold pain from cracked nipples or an aching heart. You don't want to capture the insecurity and keep it, do you?

When I look back on my first few weeks as a parent, it takes on a sepia tone. We were discovering a new world as parents. Calling each other 'Mum' and 'Dad' to see how it felt escaping our lips. Those days seem so far away now.

When we used to playfully make grabs for the buggy because we both wanted to push it. When we would make excuses to hold our baby as he slept. *I think he stirred*, we would say, a smile forming.

We pulled a mattress in front of our TV in the first giddy Eddie days. My husband took three weeks off work (but got called back after two weeks and seriously considered quitting his job because of it — anyone who thinks fathers don't feel pain at leaving their children in those early days is wrong). We camped together, us three. Learning how to be with each other.

Almost four years have passed since those days in the living room — the warmest room in our tiny flat. I don't have to miss them because life is still full of those special moments.

Now we lie with our second baby — a plump and delicious toddler now — in between us. We live in a house now. Our flat was still a home, and this one is, too. But we no longer have to camp in the lounge.

In the morning our baby, who used to fit into the crook of an arm, leaps in between us, almost squashing his brother in the process. The little one squeals with delight to see his big brother. They both dissolve into giggles as their daddy tickles them. We exchange tired looks across the golden-haired heads of our babies.

They are the constant reminder of the gratitude for this life we have. These lives we hold so precious and dear.

We don't need a ticking clock. These days are still magical. There is wonder in the ordinary.

We can look back and know that life might be busier now, but we still know we have those soft and gentle moments.

Two became three and now we're four. And time doesn't steal these moments from us. We hold them in our hearts.

BIG BOYS

The first time they tell you 'the big boys said' it will break your heart.

Curled up awkwardly in a little-boy bed, trying to convince my three-year-old son that all the world is asleep, he told me about what some big boys said. 'They called me weird. They said my clothes is funny. And they tease me for my pink gummies. They say pink is a girl's thing. Am I weird?'

I held my breath, wishing I knew what I'm meant to say. Do I say that yes, you're weird but so am I and all the best people are weird? Do I say you're not weird! You're perfect. You're the best shining star in my sky. Do I say that they're wrong, that they're mean?

I felt unprepared. But also like I should have known how to respond. That a more capable mother would know. And I felt small again, like I did at school when I was the last one picked for the game that I didn't even want to play. I don't want him to feel that. I want him to be the child who makes friends easily — the child everyone likes.

And then I realise he *is* that. He is a very loved little boy, who is adored and cherished by his friends. He has been beautifully embraced, surrounded by the wonderfully intense relationships formed by little beings. It's just his friends aren't big boys.

And then he says there's one boy who Eddie says calls Eddie a big boy and isn't that funny? Because Eddie is a big boy when he's with this little boy.

And I kind of have it then — I tell him he's going to become the big boy he wants to be friends with. You're a big boy to some and you're going to teach them what big boys are:

Big boys are kind and big boys are patient.

Big boys don't tease about pink gummies.

They celebrate difference and they never say that someone's clothes are funny unless they mean someone's clothes are *so much fun!*

They don't call people weird if being called weird hurts their feelings.

But they're weird sometimes and that's OK because it's OK to be weird. It's great to be weird!

Eddie quickly joined in. Big boys make you feel happy in your smile! They keep you safe like if you run on the road they say stop! Big boys help with the sandpit and they let you have a turn with the big spade. Big boys know all the numbers and the colours, and they push you on the swing real, real high, as high as the sky. Big boys are very clever . . .

And I pick up quickly — Big boys are very clever because they know that there's no such thing as boy things and girl things.

Yes! Eddie says — all of our things are things together.

And he pulls my hand to his face. He presses his cheek to it. I want to be a big boy, he says.

You'll be a big boy, my darling.

And you'll be kind.

I turn off the light and give one last look to the little bump in the bed who will one day grow into a big boy and then after that a teenager and then a man. And at every stage he will have the choice to be kind.

As all the world is sleeping he says in the dark — 'I'll be a kind one, dear Mama.'

BE THAT MUM

Be that mum who pulls out her phone and shows off photos of her child.

Be that mum who tells stories about her child, who talks about all of the exciting things they're doing — the milestones, the ordinary, wondrous things, the funny stories, the sad bits.

Be that mum who tears up describing how delightful her kid is.

Be that mum who proudly talks about the crafts she set up for her child, or the lunchbox that looks like a piece of art, or the way she handled an argument and turned it into a teaching moment.

Be the mum who never says she's *just* a mum.

Be the mum who champions other mums. Be the mum who supports other mums and tells them they should share and rejoice and be proud!

Parenting is something to be proud of. Don't let anyone tell you otherwise.

Don't just let slurs like 'breeder' slide. Don't nod along when people try to say mums have it easy. That they're annoying because they talk about their kids too much, or share too many photos, or don't do *enough*.

Don't let anyone make mums smaller.

Parenthood is a hard slog.

And you have every right — *every right* — to feel joy and pride about the job you're doing.

Day in and day out, you're taking care of your child — making memories, getting shit done, being better, learning more. You're kicking ass. Doing a job that is really, really worthy and valid.

This idea that parenting is nothing is straight-up harmful.

It stops parents from being able to talk about their day and celebrate their wins and reflect on what they've learned.

Working nine-to-five in an office can be boring as hell, but we don't shame people for talking about work or celebrating that they've got a promotion or have just finished a project.

Every day you parent you're doing something special. Without breaking out into a Whitney Houston hit, it's a real big fucking deal! We are shaping minds to build a better world for us all.

We need to rebel against the devaluing of what we all do. It takes guts to be a parent. It's hard. It's thankless a lot of the time. And it's *important*. Really important. We need to say no to people saying that *domestic* work — the work done mostly by women — isn't important, isn't special, isn't worth celebrating.

It is absolutely worth celebrating. And every time we celebrate, every time we stand up and say *being a mum matters*, and every time we open up about what it means for all of us — we are saying caring for future generations is important, it's valuable, it's needed and it's special.

You don't have to hide how much you love this job you've got. You don't have to keep quiet about the days that nearly break you.

Nobody else is expected to suffer in silence like mums are.

So open up. Talk about your day. Your day matters as much as anyone else's.

IT HAS BEEN A DAY

My day started at 4 a.m. today because my three-year-old thinks his insides are coming out when he vomits. He caught that bug that is going around so I woke to vomiting and screaming and he was just puking everywhere and I was gagging because I can handle poos and wees but there's something about vomit, it's just so much. I turned on the light and it was like a horror show. And I was gagging and trying to get his PJs off and they were all slimy and he was trying to hug me and I was trying to one-arm hug him because I want to comfort him but also *heave* there is vomit everywhere OMG it was in his hair. And then he puked on me. So I put him in the shower and I got in too and I kept thinking as he puked in my arms that I'm going to get the bug too because it's on me. And I sat on a stool that was meant to be for him and he sat on my lap and cried and puked and I stroked his hair and tried not to puke. And then the stool snapped under my weight because it is made for a child and it is plastic and it is not made for a giant woman covered in a three-year-old and a three-year-old's puke. And it made a big bang. And then I made a bang as I landed on the floor of the shower. And that woke the baby and then the baby was like WHY IS EVERYONE AWAKE? because usually he likes to wake on the hour every hour all night and it was 4.30 a.m. by this time so he was confused and ANGRY. So he was banging on the bathroom door because he wanted in on the 'vomit and broken chair and me laying on the floor of the shower groaning as my three-year-old said "I'm weeing"' action. He also wanted to be on my lap vomiting and/or peeing on me. And he has just learned how to say 'Mama', and the first 380 times were so cute but now for 48 hours it's just been MAMA MAMA MAMA MAMA MAMA MAMA MAMA MAMA and I was like oh, that's right. And so he was banging on the door yelling MAMA MAMA and screaming and my big boy was vomiting and screaming and my husband was like 'I have put out my back or something' and I was like WHAT? WHY IS THIS HAPPENING NOW? And then I got the kids dressed and clean(ish) and my husband was hobbling around unable to help but trying to so I helped the situation by yelling at him. And then I put on *Postman Pat* and didn't have a drink at 5.45 a.m. And then I left the chundering big baby with my broke-back husband and went to get the baby's sleep-deprivation test at the hospital. And she put the little wire things on his head and he was so calm and I said, 'Oh thank goodness he isn't screaming!' and then he screamed for an hour. Because I said that. And she said, 'Do you think you can get him to sleep?' and I thought that was the funniest joke ever. But she wasn't joking. And then I shushed so much I almost broke a blood vessel in my eye. In my eye. And then he fell asleep and it was so beautiful I almost cried. And then she said, 'OK, we have got it!' And started unbandaging him and he was suddenly screaming like he was being tortured and I was like REALLY? WE HAD TO WAKE HIM AFTER 10 MINUTES. REALLY?? IS THAT REALLY A THING WE HAD TO DO REALLY? And then my tummy started to feel sore and I was, like, please if there is any type of god please do not let me shit my pants at the hospital when I'm wearing maternity leggings that are worn through the crotch anyway. And then she said, 'Shall we wash him?' and I was already half way out the door, like NO. BUT THANK YOU. BUT I JUST NEED TO GO. And then I got outside and the feeling passed and the baby was quiet so I went and bought some baby oil which apparently is what you use to get the glue out of their hair. And then I got picked up by my hunched-over husband and the big baby with a big red bowl and he smiled and said, 'I did so much sick out in my mouf' and my husband gave me this weak smile and I gave him a kiss on the cheek which I hope said 'I'm sorry for yelling at you and I hope you're OK but we can talk about it later because kids etc.' and then the baby screamed all the way home. And then when we got home I was rocking the baby and I thought my head was going to explode and Eddie came over and said 'Please can I have a cuggle becorst mine tummy is so sore' and so we all got into bed — the baby, the big baby and the bright red bowl. And I lay down with them and sang to them a little song about having gastro to the tune of 'Paradise City': 'take me away from the very sore tummy where the poos and wees are not very funny'. And they stopped whimpering and giggled and then they cuddled up and everything was quiet and I thought, I need to get up and write and work and do the washing and clean the toilet and make the beds fresh again and then I just . . . didn't. And then I heard giggling and it was two and a half hours later and two little blond cherubs looked up at me and one said 'MAMA MAMA' and then the other started copying 'MAMA MAMA' and I kissed them both and then I thought about all the puke and I felt really gross so I quickly got up. But Eddie said 'Please another kiss on mine face dear Mama' and so I did give him another kiss on each hot, pink, flushed cheek. And I saw the baby's hair and thought shit. And so I got the baby oil and I stripped him down and put the baby oil in his hair and he yanked it out of my hand and it went everywhere and I tried to pick him up but he was naked and covered in baby oil and he thought this was so funny and he made a dash for it and I tried to grab the slippery naked baby and every step he took he farted and screamed with laughter and then the big one started to try to take his clothes off and said 'Can I be naked and cover in dat stuff too and you chased me dear Mama?' and I was like sweating and covered in baby oil and THIS IS NOT

A GAME. I threw the towel over the slimy baby and grabbed a leg but slipped again and both children jumped on me like hahaha this is so funny, try to break her. And then my older one said 'Your tummy is like a jumping castle becorst you are so soft and bouncy' and I tried to get up and the crotch of my leggings just ripped right out. And then the big baby vomited on the floor. So I put them both in the shower and gave them the bottle of baby oil and they slid around in there for a while and I sat on the ground in my ripped leggings all sweaty and gross and I felt like I was going to cry and then the baby farted. And we just all burst out laughing. Hysterical, maniacal laughter. Because farts are funny. And a baby that already looks like a leg of ham covered in baby oil like a greasy piglet is funny. And even vomit is funny sometimes. And also this is life. And it's our life. Our precious, wonderful, stupid, amazing, ridiculous life. And I never thought I'd sit in vomit in ripped-crotch leggings and try to catch naked babies covered in baby oil in a bathroom that stinks of farts and laugh this much. I never thought I'd do all those things and then still be 100 per cent sure I'm living the life I've always wanted and loving it so much. So much. I climbed into the shower and sat down and my two babies climbed into my lap and kissed my cheeks and kissed each other and I thought, that's being a mum. And in that moment I thought: I am very, very lucky.

THE CRÈCHE THAT BUILT A FAMILY

When I want my children to understand something — a concept, a word, a theme — but I struggle to work out how to explain it, I tell a story.

So here's a story . . .

It begins with a little crèche. It has three central characters, and a fourth that comes much later.

First there is a little boy.

He has an infectious laugh and sunshine in his eyes and a condition that has made it difficult for him to breathe. He has been through a lot in his short life. Surgeries, invasive procedures, poking and prodding, stays in a cold and sterile unit, and a warmer but sometimes unkind ward.

A little boy who was born into much love and hope.

Two parents — like any other parents. When their son was born they gazed at him and fought over who would push the buggy because they just wanted to keep staring at their precious bundle. Like so many parents, they doted on their baby, read him stories, sung him songs. He was their world.

And they struggled with his illness. We imagine so many things while we carry our babies in our bellies but we don't imagine that they'll be sick.

They struggled to be advocates and to love each other under stress — but they were and they did.

And they felt isolated and alone a lot of the time. And when they saw other parents who had lived in that world that they lived in — that world of beautiful children who faced so many challenges so beautifully — they fell over their words trying to connect. Like a light switching on, they clung to people who knew what it was like.

But their world felt very small.

And their precious little boy would lean against the big wide window and look out to the world and say 'Out!' And they struggled to try to bring the world to him.

Then good news, because this is a happy story. They were told that the little boy was getting better, but it was tinged with a note of warning. Be careful. And they always were, so careful.

So they thought about a place where a little boy could go where they would understand. That hope, with the sombre note . . . It was important they understood just how precious their baby was.

Down the winding steps, behind the church, they thought — will this be the place?

It was small, and small is what they needed. But it wasn't just that.

When they walked in, the little boy ran to where the children sat around a woman whose love for children was as clear as the bright, cold sky outside.

In this warm room they sang and they included the little boy in their song and he beamed at his mummy and daddy and they bit their lips and looked at each other and tried very hard not to let any tears fall.

This might be the place they said to each other without any words.

Another teacher put her hand on the mummy's shoulder and she knew, too. This was a moment.

This is the place they knew.

And on the first day of Little School — which is what they

called it to the boy with big blue eyes and golden hair — they took photos. Photos of his excited grin and his backpack and his daddy's look of love and pride and something else . . .

In their eyes was a brightness, of hope, but also fear.

They were scared of colds and snotty noses and sore throats that might mean long stays in hospital, but they had been told it was a good time to try. They needed time, too — to rebuild the home that can break sometimes under the stress of a condition with many syllables.

And when they left him, that first day, and he walked away holding the hands of the teachers who already seemed to love him, they knew it was the right choice.

A few hours, a few short days, a week — it might not seem like much but it is so much, it was so much.

And as the weeks went on, beautiful things began to happen.

This is the boy the crèche built.

The boy is brave and strong. He was already that — but now he gets to be brave and strong for others.

The boy is confident and proud and independent.

The boy is happy and friendly and delighted by the world inside the walls of the little home down the winding stairs behind the church.

For once his story is more than just an illness which people struggled to overlook before. In the walls inside the little home down the winding stairs behind the church the little boy is so much more than the little boy with the breathing problem.

This is the mummy the crèche built.

The mummy feels there is hope.

The mummy gets to have a community around her that isn't burdened by a past that is too painful to talk about.

The mummy sees a future and she is filled with light.

This is the daddy the crèche built.

The daddy is reassured his son is safe.

The daddy gets to reconnect with the world that felt far away.

The daddy's shoulders aren't so tight, and those broad shoulders are home to the mummy again.

This is the family the crèche built.

A fourth little member joins the fold. A beloved younger brother.

Because the little crèche down the winding stairs behind the church taught the family that days are always changing and there's a whole world out there. That sometimes it's scary but, with a community around you, you won't walk alone.

The little crèche helped raise a little boy but it also raised two parents, too.

And it wasn't the crèche, four walls, and a roof — it was the teachers.

Teachers who love children that aren't theirs, but are. Teachers who may never know the impact they've had on lives. Teachers who are a window to the world that a little boy presses his head against. A wish, a prayer — brought to life by a kind and gentle voice.

Teachers who build confidence and resilience and through that build solid foundations for families to learn how to be families.

This is the story of my family, and like all good stories it comes with a happy ending.

But not just one. Every day when the little boy smiles, we are reminded of where he has learned that confidence, the smiles he has traded with sandy hands and dirt smudges in golden hair, and splodges of paint behind little ears.

Once upon a time there was a crèche that was a home that built a family, because of the kindness and love of the teachers — who never gave up on the parents of a little boy who needed just a little bit of extra help.

Because sometimes we all need a little help. A hand on a

shoulder. A smile to get us through.

This is a story for all of the teachers who do this — may you know the impact you make in the world. The smiles you made. The love you gave.

The homes you built.

DEVELOPMENTAL MILESTONES FOR PARENTS

eeee

First time you sleep longer than 45 minutes.

First time you wear pants that don't have an elastic waist.

First time you get to have sex without having to stop halfway through because the baby is crying.

First time you get to drink an entire glass of wine without falling asleep after two sips.

First time you go out without ringing home for an update.

First time you sleep through the night. (It's not always when they do!)

First time you get to eat a whole meal without sharing any of it.

First time you drink a coffee while it's still hot.

First time you brush your hair and/or don't put it up in a 'mum bun'.

HERE'S TO THE DADS AND THE MAMAS

Here's to the dads who get stuck in bright yellow plastic tunnels at parks around the world.

Here's to the dads at ballet class mustering all the grace they can as they try to pirouette.

Here's to the dads who know all the words to 'Let It Go' and don't mind being Anna when they'd rather be Elsa.

Here's to the mamas who fish the remote control out of the toilet.

Here's to the mamas who remember the names of all of the kindy teachers.

Here's to the mamas who know when vaccinations are due and always remember to keep a treat in their bag for when it's needed.

Here's to the dads getting up before their babies so they can make lunches.

Here's to the dads looking skyward in prayer as they tackle another load of washing.

Here's to the mamas up late at night paying bills and working on budgets.

Here's to the mamas taking care of business and nailing that daycare drop-off with no tears.

Here's to the dads feeling overwhelmed as they rock their baby to sleep as they scream for boobs.

Here's to the mamas who fix their child's broken go-cart.

Here's to all the mamas and the dads and the papas and the mummies. We make our own way as parents. We do our best for our children and we try to show them the way. We play to our strengths and we work on our weaknesses. Oh, how we work. We work for our babies and for our future and we keep going. And that's the gift we give them.

Raise a glass for all the unsaid work. The times when there should have been a thank-you but there wasn't. The times you tried so hard and it went unnoticed.

Your efforts will be noticed one day, though — the first time you see your child help another. The first time they act with love and compassion. The way they continue to act with grace and kindness.

You've done that.

When your child, strong and confident, turns to you one day with recognition in their eyes — you'll know then that all of those times when it all felt so hard, it was worth it.

Maybe one day you'll look at them on their graduation, or the day they introduce you to the person they love, when they hold their baby in their arms, when they have their first day at a new job and ring you to tell you all about it. When they tell you about their first heartbreak. The first time they feel really low.

And you'll know then, that every time you dried a tear it wasn't the last time and it was worth it.

Every time you gave a high-five or your heart swelled with pride? You'll have that again and again.

Here's to the mamas and the dads who never stop.

Who wouldn't ever want to stop.

AT THE ZOO

At the zoo Eddie was entranced by the vet. She explained how the kererū had been rescued and nursed back to health. He loves kererū. He is fascinated by the creatures he sees at the zoo. He loves that there's a 'hosdiddle jus for aminals'.

The vet turned to her entranced audience and asked: 'Does anyone have a question?'

Eddie's hand shot up. He raced toward the button that allows you to talk to the vets in the sterile room.

'What's your question, buddy?' she asked him.

'How are you today?' Eddie said.

TO MY SON'S TEACHER

Thank you for noticing. I don't know how you did it. But you did.

So many children tugging at your pant leg and wrapping themselves around you and parents trying to get your attention and teachers asking you questions and somehow you saw me.

You saw me struggling to get my son's stupid bag into the stupid cubby hole. You saw me looking up at the ceiling as he began to cry. He didn't want me to leave but I needed to, I really needed to leave. For so many reasons.

And you saw me quickly spin around to see where the baby had crawled off to. And you saw me in silent prayer. You saw me angrily wipe at my eyes, my cheeks flushed.

I don't know how you did it — drop-off is so chaotic. But at a time when I felt like I was disappearing, you saw me. When I felt like I wasn't here, you made sure I knew I wasn't invisible.

Maybe it's your years of experience working in these homes-away-from-home. Maybe you've seen a lot of mothers like me. Mothers who aren't coping.

You saw me pick up my baby and sit heavily on the couch. You saw me search for kind words for my three-year-old. You saw me looking up to hide tears that were threatening to fall again. You saw me breathing deeply. Maybe I was gasping.

And you came to me and smiled and gave me a hug — and it shocked me. I thought I was hiding this. I'd hid it for weeks now. But you saw through my crappy disguise.

And you talked to me.

And you didn't give me a hollow talk that begins and ends

with 'If there's anything we can do to help . . .'

You just told me what we were going to do. And I needed that so much.

I needed so much for someone to tell me how to get through this bad spot. This dark and shitty time. I was so tired I felt like I was in quicksand and you saw me and you reached out a hand.

I needed someone who wouldn't give me an out, who wouldn't let me straight away dismiss valid concerns with 'Oh I'm fine, it's nothing.'

Thank you for your insistence.

Sometimes, when we are in it — when we're in that very bad place, even if it's just a short visit — we can't see that we're there. We don't recognise the surroundings, and the day-to-day is so relentless that we can't see that everything has changed.

So many people don't have the gift of firstly, being able to see this in others, but secondly, being able to do something about it. It takes courage to reach out. Especially when everyone is already trying to get your attention.

You did something. And you did it just at the right time. I did need help to get through that period of horrific sleep deprivation. I did need help to acknowledge how over-worked and over-stretched I was. But I wouldn't have seen it if you hadn't sat down with me and helped me.

I want you to know now that we are thriving. The breaks you gave us by enrolling our other son and pushing me to give up my guilt and shame and *do something* worked. Doing something gave us our life back. I slept. Finally. And every minute of sleep brought me back to the real world.

He loved kindergarten, as you knew he would. And we all had time to breathe again.

And we began to cope again. And it was so quick — the light was there and we were at the end of the tunnel. Just like that!

You gave us permission to feel overwhelmed and to do

something about it. You gave us permission to acknowledge that sleep deprivation was kind of killing us. And you handed us a solution.

And my gosh, we are grateful. Grateful doesn't even begin to cut it.

So thank you. Again. For noticing what others might not have. How you ever looked upon that crazy scene and somehow zeroed in on me and saw, I'll never know.

I can see that you view your job as being more than raising children. You're raising families and you're making sure nobody falls through the cracks. That no family is swallowed up.

You're a mother yourself and maybe that's where your empathy comes from.

Your home is called a Learning Community and I see a lot of learning but it's not just numbers and letters.

I see confidence being taught, not just to children but to adults, too. Important life lessons about advocating not just for our children but for ourselves as mothers. Learning that we need to look after ourselves, too, not just our children.

You taught me a vital lesson and I wasn't expecting it.

We all have a breaking point. We can all only hope that if we ever reach rock bottom, there's someone to help us up.

Thank you for helping us.

Thank you for teaching in every sense of the word. For welcoming us into your community and showing such compassion and kindness.

It means more than you'll ever know, and I know now that I can do the same for another mother. And it brings me great comfort to know you've done this for others, and you'll keep doing it for many more.

Love,
the mum who cried at drop-off

THE JUST FUCKING DOING IT CLUB

When I was pregnant with my first baby I would often ring my sister and bitch and whine about how tired I was and how hard everything was and how I hated being pregnant. I absolutely cringe about it now, because I literally moaned about being pregnant (kind of relentlessly) to another pregnant woman who already had a child to look after.

There's a hierarchy around complaining when you're pregnant (and also around sleep — as in, if you wake up once a night I don't want to hear about it, go tell someone whose kid is sleeping through the night) and as I wasn't a parent yet (and I was also a dick) I didn't get this.

My sister is a very patient woman. Particularly when it comes to me. Which is handy given how much I must test her patience.

On one of the days when I moaned to her (and to make matters a hell of a lot worse she was *very* pregnant and ill and I was just a bit pregnant and ill), I said to her, 'I don't know how you do it. There's no way I could cope without being able to nap as soon as I get home from work.'

I just . . . what a dick. Honestly. I was such a dick.

Not taking my sister's sigh as a polite shut-the-hell-up-now I decided to double-down and say: 'Really, how do you do it? I would just be so tired!'

Helpful!

Then, and it's stuck with me ever since, my sister said, 'I don't know, you just do it, it's not like anybody else is going to do it for you.'

At the time I was really committed to being annoying, so I just said some more annoying stuff like WELL I AM JUST SO TIRED I THINK I'LL HAVE A NAP! YOU SHOULD HAVE ONE, TOO!

Luckily, in response to that she didn't even yell or anything (she was probably too tired, or quite used to me being annoying).

Fast-forward to my being pregnant with my second baby and running after my first and one day at work someone said to me: 'I don't know how you do it! I get so tired when I have a late night and I'm not even pregnant!'

And my sister's words came back to me.

Every time someone says 'I don't know how you do it!' or 'You must be exhausted! How do you cope?' or any variation of this, I hear my sister's voice and I just think:

You just fucking do it. You just do.

And you know what? It is fucking impressive but also it is what it is.

We are the Just Fucking Doing It Club.

Nobody gets shit done like mothers do. The fierce determination, the focused energy, the quiet and methodical mahi of parenting — mums are killing it.

When you've got to work because nobody else is going to pay the damn bills.

When you've got to get through that kindy drop-off because shit has to get done.

When you've got to get through the day with a fucking smile (or 8000 smiles) after three hours' sleep.

When you've got to get the lunches done even though you'd rather be watching *House of Cards* and having complex feelings about whether or not you'd sleep with Kevin Spacey if you were really drunk and somehow a Washington intern.

When you've got to get to a Plunket appointment then to Rock 'n' Rhyme and get six loads of washing done then make your midwife appointment and entertain your toddler in the waiting room for 40 minutes.

When you've got to finish the newsletter for your kid's co-op while your toddler tries to maim himself by climbing up the pantry shelves.

When you've got to somehow get the baby to realise Pamol isn't poison so you can bring down a temperature while you try to make a doctor's appointment but you keep getting put on hold.

When you've got to fix the wheel on the buggy and make sure the baby doesn't chew through the cord for the TV.

When you've got to sort the phone bill and pair up all the socks and listen to your three-year-old's complex story that ends with 'SO WHY DON'T YOU HAVE BALLS, DEAR MAMA?'

When you're sure you've got nothing left and you just want five fucking minutes but that's not going to happen because your baby needs to watch you poo — like, seriously, they seem to need this more than anything they've ever needed before.

When you've missed the fucking bus or your car needs a warrant of fitness and you have to get to a job interview.

MAMAS ARE JUST FUCKING DOING IT.

No matter how shit the sleep was, no matter how exhausting the morning was, no matter how hard it was to get the kids out the door to start the day — mamas are just fucking doing it.

And they're doing it with grace and love and compassion.

When they've got nothing left to give, mamas are still giving.

Giving to their kids.

Giving to their partners.

Giving to their family.

Giving to their friends.

Giving to their community.

So on the days when everything goes wrong, on the mornings after the nights that were agony, in the middle of the afternoon when you're so tired you feel like it hurts to move — remember, you're doing it. You're fucking doing it even when you feel like you're a failure. You're not.

Look at you — you're fucking doing it.

I know it feels sometimes like you're not doing it well. I know it feels like everyone else is doing it better. I know you want to be the best mum you can be.

You're fucking doing it.

When the kids are crying and you're overwhelmed, remember: you're fucking doing it. Right now, right here, you're getting shit done and you're just fucking doing it.

This life is you, you've made it and you're making it.

Never forget that. When you get a chance to stop and drink some cold coffee or tea, if the kids get to sleep and you get to pour a glass of wine or, fuck it, a gin, make sure you take a moment and say:

FUCK YEAH. I'M FUCKING DOING IT.

You're doing it so well that everyone around you is just, like, how does she do it? How does she cope?

And you can stand up and say:

I just fucking do it.

And, just so you know — you do it really fucking well.

THE PAINTING

Looking at a new painting Eddie had brought home from kindy I said:

That's gorgeous, bunny! What is it?

I NOT A BUNNY. I AM A EDDIE.

OK, sorry Eddie, what is it?

IT A PAINTING!!

Oh, I know, but what is it?

He sighed deeply and looked at me as if I was the most simple being to grace the planet.

IT PAINT ON A PAPER DEAR MAMA. WHAT AM YOUR EYES FOR?

HOW TO GET YOUR CHILD TO EAT THEIR DINNER

Place meal in front of them.

* Insist veges are not touching each other.
* Wipe away sauce and put it on a new, separate plate.
* Put all food onto a different plate.
* Explain that it definitely is sausage and they do in fact like sausage because they asked for sausage for dinner.
* Say 'Just try one bite' six to eight thousand times.
* Offer a piece of cheese.
* Remove cheese from wrapper.
* Listen to child explain that they can't eat the cheese because you removed the wrapper when they wanted to remove it.
* Eat disgusting cheese from wrapper. Give child piece of cheese with wrapper still on.
* Take deep breath as child asks you to unwrap cheese. Then pray to all gods old and new for strength when they say they can't eat the cheese because you unwrapped it.
* Try bribery. For example, 'If you eat your potato I will dress up as Fireman Sam and burp the theme tune for your enjoyment.'
* Make new meal.
* Perform 40-minute interpretive dance to encourage them to eat the new meal.
* Check Facebook group thread about how to get your

child to eat and read first comment that says 'I'd never make a new meal for my child. Mothers who do that are creating self-absorbed narcissistic bed-wetters who will never leave home.'

* Feel terrible.
* Lose will to live.
* Say 'Well, you need to stay at the dinner table until you've eaten something.'
* Accept defeat two days later when you're still at the dinner table and they still haven't eaten anything.
* Say 'Well, what would you like to eat then?'
* Scream silently when they say 'sausage'.

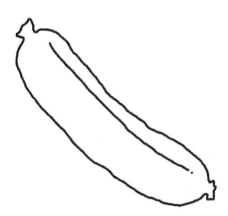

MOTHERING BOYS

I get asked a lot about raising boys, so here's my two cents:

Boys! Oh my gosh! My house is absolutely full of princess crap and it drives me up the wall! I feel like everything is pink and glittery and covered in tulle! It's a nightmare.

I am not a princess person. I only wear two colours — black and very black. So to have a house taken over by various shades of pink does my head in!

My son is obsessed with Elsa so I hear 'Let It Go' 800 million times a day. (You feel my pain, don't you? You know what it's like, mother of sons!)

On Sundays we do ballet — tutus in every colour and flower crowns that look like they've been chewed on by a pitbull.

Duplo towers everywhere! Those bloody Matchbox cars — the wheels always fall off and then they're upset about the wheels and they want me to fix it and I'm like, kid, that is a $2 car. Just throw it in the bin.

But they can't because cars are precious. And rocks are precious. And their baby with a face covered in felt-tip pen that they feed with a little pretend bottle is precious. And their necklace that they made with misshapen beads and painted bits of elbow pasta is precious.

Both my boys cannot sit still. My oldest talks *so much*. To everyone. To himself. To the dog. And I'm pretty sure the dog is deaf.

They both always lose their socks.

My baby laughs really loudly — mums of boys, you hear me, don't you? Boys laugh so loud! And they say **MAMA MAMA** all the time.

And what about all the best-friend drama? Every day there's a new best friend and they're not my best friend anymore and I need one of those CSI wall diagrams with bits of string linking each child to work out who I am meant to invite over for a playdate.

My baby loves putting things into things, like little people into little cars and pegs into buckets and paper into baskets and boxes into littler boxes.

Boys, am I right?

They both love tea sets and the colour green. And they can spend hours in the sandpit or playing babies!

I mean, you know what boys are like — I can barely get mine off his bike long enough to re-tie his baby carrier that holds his baby that for some unknown reason he named Elephine. Creepy, creepy Elephine with the bung eyes.

BOYS!

The baby constantly wants to turn the light on and off and he cannot look at a roll of toilet paper without unrolling it. Such a boy compulsion.

My oldest boy loves to paint and make cards that say 'Thank You' and 'I Love You' and he loves to rip up paper and make a mess and I have to always say *'Ew don't do that, it's disgusting.'*

Every time we see a face painter my son wants to be a butterfly or a fairy or a street sweeper or an industrial vacuum cleaner.

My boys are very delicate and gentle and loud and boisterous and cuddly and angry and delighted and easily upset and resilient and quiet and hilarious and rambunctious.

My oldest boy will only eat chicken nuggets. Unless it's a high tea, of course.

My youngest boy will only eat every single thing you put in front of him.

I mean, boys! They're such boys.

Fairies and princesses and queens and dragons and Mr Potato Head and going to the beach and getting covered in mud and ballet and playing rock-star guitar and books about farts and tea parties and saying poo bum wees penis balls and cuddles and singing 'You Are My Sunshine' and little kisses on noses and gentle pats for the cat and trucks that need to smash and blowing bubbles.

Such boys.

Mums of boys understand! They're just so different to girls! *So different!*

wink

TOP 5 THINGS THAT MADE MY 14-MONTH-OLD CRY TODAY

1. Existing.
2. Being almost asleep.
3. Being awake.
4. Being in the car.
5. Not being in the car.

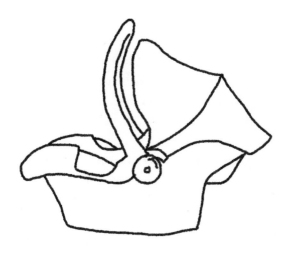

A WORD FOR THIS

They need a word to describe the utter devastation you feel when your child cries the second you leave their room after you've spent 58 minutes patting and shushing them and you were absolutely sure they were asleep but now they're standing up in their cot screaming at you.

They need a word for the desire for a coffee or anything with caffeine in it after a night of so many wake-ups you stopped counting.

They need a word for the feeling you get when you toast a crumpet for your toddler and they say 'Can I have honey?' and you give them honey and then they say 'I meant butter' and you decide to be nice and make them a new one with butter and they say 'Oh, I meant honey' and smile sweetly, and you want to put your head in the oven.

They need a word for the look that old ladies give you in the supermarket when your threenager throws the most epic tantrum of all time and all you can think about is when they were born and old ladies used to look at you like you were the queen or the second coming.

They need a word for the noise of an indoor playground during school holidays — it's made by what sounds like thousands of screaming children but in reality is somehow only 30.

They need a word for the lie that you tell the nurse at check-up when they ask if you've ever let the baby sleep in your bed.

They need a word for the nod you give that nosy aunt who keeps asking if you've started solids yet when your baby is three days old.

They need a word for the reason why you still greet your baby with a smile in the morning when you're exhausted and they're the ones who kept you up all night, a word for the shoulder squeeze you give your partner when they yawn at the sink, a word for the grateful sigh you give a friend who offers to watch the baby so you can sleep, a word for the tears you cry in the shower because you're so overwhelmed but you're also so happy, a word for that feeling when you first hold your baby in your arms after waiting for them for nine months . . .

Oh, they've got a word for that . . .

Love.

A LITTLE OUTING

I remember a time when I wanted to go somewhere. And I just went there.

Now I have children.

Every time I want to go out with said children, an ordeal begins. It goes something like this . . .

Step 1: Decide you want to go out.

Step 2: Check calendar to see if you can go out. You don't have anything else to do until your Plunket appointment in three hours! You can definitely make it out! Three hours is *loads* of time to get ready and go and have a coffee somewhere!

Step 3: Change nappy in preparation for excursion into actual real world.

Step 4: Feel charge of excitement and anxiety over venturing beyond your house. Could it be? Will you make it out? A coffee! You could talk to another person!

Step 5: Imagine talking to a real person that has an age that's more than a single digit.

Step 6: Break into a sweat.

Step 7: Put on your best post-maternity leggings.

Step 8: Look for a hairbrush.

Step 9: Give up after 10 minutes. Where did those kids put it? It's your third hairbrush this month? Why are they hoarding hairbrushes? It's not like they enjoy getting their hair brushed.

Step 10: Pack a jumper for each child in case it gets cold, a singlet for each child in case it gets warmer. A hat and sunscreen. Another hat in case you lose the first hat because your baby keeps pulling it off and throwing it on the floor. Pack socks, a pair of pants and a pair of shorts. Pack three bibs. Throw in a fourth for good measure.

Step 11: Consider swapping already enormous nappy bag for bag on wheels.

Step 12: Make a lunchbox of snacks. Provide at least 15 different types of snacks so that your fussy child has a variety of things to throw on the floor.

What's that smell?

Step 13: Change nappy again. Add an extra nappy to the nappy bag. Pause. Add another four nappies. If only the baby slept as often as they poop.

Get interrupted by three-year-old.

Step 14: Encourage them to wee. Listen to impassioned eight-minute speech by precious precocious first-born about how they don't need to pee, have never ever needed to pee, you can't make them pee, you're a mean mummy, they don't want to go out anyway, they won't go to the toilet no matter what not ever no never ever, are we going to the park? They only want to go to the park. You're not their best friend. You're their best friend. But they need their other shorts. Not those ones, the other ones. They're a baby dinosaur, OK. Say it. Say 'Goodnight, baby dinosaur'.

Step 15: Say 'Goodnight, baby dinosaur.'

Step 16: Spend 10 minutes trying to get oldest child to put on shorts. Give up. Let them wear tutu with rugby shorts underneath, bow tie, pink gumboots, fairy wings, leg-warmers, and a dinosaur apron with Fireman Sam hat.

Step 17: They will not go to the toilet.

Step 18: *Where is the baby?* Find baby in the shower covered in soap. Change baby into new outfit.

Step 19: Hustle children to the car. This takes at least 20 minutes and includes the following questions:

Mum, what is sun?

But why?

What is yellow?

Why is yellow?

Am I a leaf?

Why is this?

Can a volcano eat a raincoat?

What is air?

Step 20: Bribe them with pretzels. Feel guilty for bribing them with food. Consider that maybe you've given them food issues forever. They're going to hate you when they're older and you will have to pay for their therapy. What did that lady at coffee group who seemed to have her shit together say? Don't use food as a treat?

Step 21: Eat half a block of chocolate standing by the car, crying.

Step 22: While putting three-year-old into the car seat, baby pulls open nappy bag and opens container of yoghurt and pours the contents into the nappy bag.

Step 23: Repack the nappy bag while baby cries for yoghurt. Try to ignore outraged yelling from the car as three-year-old yells at you for leaving them in their car seat.

Step 24: Put baby into car seat. Climb into front seat.

Step 25: Oldest says they need to pee.

Step 26: Take them to the toilet. They want to wear shorts. Tell them to go to their room and get changed while you check baby.

Step 27: Give baby a rusk and turn around just in time to see three-year-old emerge from the house wearing nothing but a pair of shorts, on his head.

Step 28: Change three-year-old.

Step 29: Go into temporary dream state where you remember what it was like to leave the house before children.

Step 30: Realise you have to be on the other side of town for your Plunket appointment in 13 minutes.

HEAD VS HEART

Every now and then, when I see or hold a new baby, my head and heart begin an epic battle. I know I don't want another child — yet. I mean ever. *Ever.* But maybe . . . no. See, it's even happening right here as I'm trying to write this!

My internal battle — my head-versus-heart war — sparks up regularly. Just a few days ago while holding my friend's darling wee boy it began, quietly at first with . . .

My Heart: *Oh, he smells so delicious.*

Oh, look at his tiny fingers. I want another baby.

And My Head: YOU WHAT? ARE YOU ON CRACK RIGHT NOW?

No, I am not on crack! I just . . . Look at him.

HE IS VERY CUTE BUT NO.

But just a little bit of a baby.

YOU HAVE A BABY RIGHT NOW. LITERALLY. YOU HAVE A BABY ALREADY.

But he is so big now. He's practically an adult when you compare him to this baby.

NO. YOU DO NOT WANT A BABY. HAVE A HOON ON THIS ONE. GIVE HIM BACK. HOLD YOUR OTHER LITERAL BABY AND STOP THIS NONSENSE.

Don't tell me what to do. Babies are precious and I'll have another five if I want to. I have always wanted a big family.

YOU HAVE NEVER WANTED A BIG FAMILY. THIS IS HORMONES AND NOTHING ELSE. WHAT ABOUT SLEEP? DON'T YOU WANT SLEEP?

Yes, but I'm not sleeping now, so how much worse could it—

HOW MUCH WORSE CAN NOT SLEEPING BE? HOW ABOUT YOU ADD TWO MORE YEARS TO THE ENTIRE TWO YEARS YOU HAVE ALREADY NOT BEEN SLEEPING? YOU WOKE 17 TIMES LAST NIGHT! YOU HAVE HAD FOUR NIGHTS OF SLEEP IN A YEAR!

Well, my new baby might sleep.

HE WILL NOT SLEEP.

It might be a little girl.

IT WILL NOT BE.

You don't know that.

I LITERALLY DO. YOU ARE BEING CRAZY. YOU NEED TO GET SOME SLEEP. OK? AND GIVE BACK THAT BABY. YOU ARE SCARING ITS MUM BY MAKING WEIRD GROANING NOISES.

He's so beautiful.

GIVE HIM BACK.

I just want to—

STOP SNIFFING HIM. YOU ARE CREEPING EVERYONE OUT. OK. EVERYONE HAS STOPPED TALKING AND YOU ARE HUFFING THAT BABY IN FRONT OF EVERYONE.

But tiny socks!

YOU HAVE THOSE ALL OVER THE DAMN HOUSE ALREADY. WOMAN. NONE OF THEM MATCH AND YOU'RE ALWAYS BITCHING ABOUT IT.

And cuddles.

AND NEVER SLEEPING.

And they hold your finger with their teeny tiny hands.

AND SCREAM FOR A VERY LONG TIME.

I just don't know if I am done yet.

YOU ARE VERY DONE AND ALSO YOU HAVE A BABY. I TOLD YOU. YOU ALREADY HAVE ONE. HIS NAME IS HAM AND HE IS A BABY.

He's a toddler! He's not this tiny and wee and liddle and smoll.

THIS NEEDS TO STOP. GIVE THE BABY BACK AND GO HAVE A LIE-DOWN. OH. THAT'S RIGHT YOU CAN'T. BECAUSE YOU ALREADY LITERALLY HAVE TWO BABIES AND NOW YOU WANT A THIRD AND THIS IS MADNESS.

My other friend, who does not have children, usually breaks up my internal yelling match by asking if anyone wants wine. And as I watch my friends with tiny babies turn down a glass, there is suddenly a winner for this round. Yes, you're right, Head.

Mama needs a wine, baby.

NOT A SAUSAGE

Goodnight, my sweet little sausage.

I AM NOT AN SAUSAGE I AM AN LIDDLE BOY CALL EDDIE YOU STOP DAT NOW.

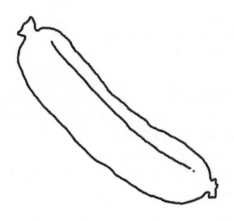

SCREEN TIME

~⌒~

The most awkward thing happened to me: I accidentally forgot to give a crap about how much screen time my kid has.

Screen time is the new evil, don't you know? Any amount of time is too much time. The Apple guy knew — he didn't let his kids use his products! Which isn't hypocritical and controlling at all.

There are TV programmes about the dangers of screen time, which seems, umm, counter-productive. There's some advertising campaign saying you need to turn your family on instead of a TV, which seems, well . . . an unfortunate choice of words . . .

Because by doing that you'll be happy and safe and maybe you'll want to drive a specific brand-that-shall-not-be-named car.

We must go back to ye old days where we all lived happily inside a Johnny Cash song. Daddy sang bass, Mama sang tenor and me and little brother would join right in there.

Wholesome family activity. Sitting around the wireless in a trouble-free patriarchal existence, just appreciating all that we had.

Not like today! With these parents who are letting their kids unwind in front of the TV as if they're adults who like to get home from work and unwind in front of the TV!

Look — between you and me and, like, the other three people reading this — I don't set any limits on screen time. Because I don't have to.

I chuck it on when I need to get stuff done. And sometimes

my son will say, 'Can I watch some *In The Night Garden*?' and I can tell he's tired and he just wants to relax. And I'll say '*In the Night Garden* is creepy as hell, but as you wish.' And I'll put it on and he will watch for a bit and then he'll go do something else.

And it just isn't an issue. It just isn't. *They* keep telling us that kids are addicted to screens and they need to get out into nature — as if it's one or the other. And they say kids are watching screens 23 hours a day and it's killing society. And there's much hand-wringing; it reminds me of when I was a kid and everyone believed video games were going to be the downfall of society. And before that, when it was TV. And before that when it was like I don't know . . . radio. And newspapers. And probably cars and not wearing loin cloths (look, I dunno, I'm not a historian).

My point is there's always something that's going to be the downfall of society. And they can insist that it's screens, but I don't think it is.

I feel very bad for screens and I am very grateful for screens. Screens are a very useful co-parent to me. Here's a short list of reasons why I love screens:

1. In the children's ward, my son watched *Fireman Sam* on an iPad and it momentarily made him feel like a normal kid who wasn't very sick in a hospital.
2. Reading my Kindle at 3 a.m. while my son was in hospital was a lifeline to me. It switched off my anxious brain. It momentarily dulled the terrified screaming loop I had running in my head.
3. My friends and community are in my phone. Being able to connect with other mums online and say 'Hey I'm at the park wanna meet me?' meant I wasn't completely isolated as a new mum. In what's arguably the most relentless job in the world, other parents are my colleagues and I talk to some of them or I organise meet-ups through a screen.

4. There are some days (a lot of days) when I'm so exhausted I feel like I could cry. And I do cry. And sometimes I just want to have a little cry about how tired I am. And I'd rather not have an audience for that — particularly not an audience of small people who I have to reassure that there's not something really wrong. A screen means I can have some space to myself . . . to take a deep breath. To get through.

5. Screens are as passive as you are. I have learned a lot about my son and what he loves and how he feels by watching things with him and talking to him about what he's watching. Elsa makes him feel strong. The monster on Sesame Street taught him to tell me when he feels overwhelmed. He loves learning te reo Māori because then he knows the words Moe from *The Moe Show* uses to describe various random things. Yes, sometimes he just sits and it is a passive activity — but a lot of the time it isn't. Yoga babies and even the monstrous Wiggles get my son up and active.

6. Screens can be a window to the world. They spark curious minds. One morning my son raced into the bedroom and said MAMA DO ELEPHANTS SWIM IN THE OCEAN!? And I was like hmmm, that is a good question. We looked it up and then watched a YouTube clip together of an elephant swimming in the ocean. It was wonderful.

There are more reasons. But let's just stop there. Screens aren't evil. There isn't a moral binary here. Everything in moderation (if he watches no TV one day then I figure he can watch seven hours the next day) and all of that rubbish.

But don't worry about being *that* parent. I'm *that* parent and screens don't scare me.

MESSY MUMMY

Today as I rushed my oldest into kindy I went to give him a kiss goodbye and saw his face was smeared with Marmite.

I looked around (somewhat wildly) for a tissue, couldn't find one, so I put my top in my mouth and then rubbed his face with it.

Then I rushed to a meeting for my job that should only be a few hours a week but actually feels like my entire week. And I looked down at my top as I arrived 15 minutes late again and I thought:

It looks like poo.

I look like I have a smear of poo on my top.

I rushed through my day in my Marmite/poo top and rushed home and took over from my husband who was looking after the baby who was snotty. As he cried at the injustice of having his cuddle with Daddy being taken over by me, he rubbed his crusty nose across the shoulder of my top.

When I walked into kindy and picked up my oldest, he said EWW. THERE'S BOOGS ON YOUR TOP. IT GREEN!

As I struggled to get his backpack shut I pulled out the lunchbox and it fell open. I perched it on the benchtop as I pulled the leg of my crawling baby, trying to stop him going near any toys with his germs.

The open half-eaten yoghurt from the lunchbox fell into my hair. I quickly dragged my sleeve through my hair to rub it in — hoping nobody would notice.

I shoved the kids into the buggy and headed to the coffee shop. I paid for my coffee and went to put my wallet back into the nappy bag. I was holding my coffee with my wallet but was somehow too scattered to notice. I managed to pour my hot coffee into the nappy bag.

I used an entire pack of baby wipes to try to soak up the mess. I rubbed my phone across my top to try to dry it, leaving a smear of brown across my chest.

I am definitely that mum. The mum who can't wear white. The mum who doesn't bother buying new clothes.

I could turn the top into a metaphor for parenting, I suppose. Make some comment about the durability of motherhood. How you selflessly sacrifice a top.

Or I could just say this:

I live in hope that one day I actually look like I have my shit together. It simply cannot be my reality that I look messier than my toddler for all of eternity!

DON'T BE SMUG

This is a cautionary tale. Learn from my mistakes. There is a rule in parenting: never, ever be smug. I'm here to tell you why.

You can't ever clock parenting. It's not a game where you get to each level and then you win. It's not a race where there's a finish line and a podium. There's no award ceremony, not even a certificate of participation (OK, maybe your kid is that!).

My point is that you can have wins along the way, but parenting is designed to get you just when you think you've mastered one aspect of it.

Case in point: me and my smugness.

Here is an incomplete list of times I have been a smug dickhead:

CLINGY BABIES

My sister was the first person close to me to become a mum and the first person I got to see actually parent. She is an amazing mum and is my mumspiration (if I was an awful person who says things like mumspiration, which sounds like a deodorant for busy mums).

When she visited me and my brand-new baby with her eight-month-old (her second baby), I remember thinking 'Gosh, he [my nephew] is clingy!' And you know, that's fine to think but I then thought (in my stupid *I totally know heaps about kids because I gave birth yesterday* kind of way), 'Well, I'm going to make sure I don't have a clingy baby. I'm not going to take them everywhere with me. If my baby cries while I'm in the shower, too bad. You need to foster independence! You're the boss! You just say — no kid, I'm going to the other room and you just need to learn to enjoy your own company.'

Such a dick. And apologies to my sister, but also she won't mind me saying this because she knows better than anyone that I was a smug dick.

My first baby wasn't clingy. Do you know why? Because he wasn't. That's it. Nothing I did made him not clingy. He was just not clingy. End of story.

My second baby looks at me like he would like to live in my uterus again. He eyes me like I'm a Big Mac and he hasn't eaten in six weeks. When I leave his line of vision (not even the room) he screams as if he's being waterboarded. He is most comfortable when he is *clinging to me like a koala on a tree in a flash flood.* Once, my husband held him in front of me while I peed. Just so he wouldn't cry. He watches me in the shower, OK?

You cannot foster independence in a baby who protests with more gusto and enthusiasm than a career anarchist at an anti-capitalist rally every time you try to put them down. I'm not the boss. He can't talk but I swear he told me that it will be a cold day in hell before he enjoys his own company.

I did nothing differently with the two kids. I now know there are clingy kids and not-clingy kids. I also know that I knew nothing.

FUSSY EATING

I am not the only dick who said that I wouldn't allow my kids to be fussy eaters. HAHAHAHA, 'allow'? Oh please. When you're actually parenting (as in *parenting*, not waxing lyrical on Twitter while you sip lattes and imagine what it will be like if one day you have kids), you realise there's no quick fix when it comes to kids and eating. I have one child who hoovers everything to the point where I can't put food on a serviette or a paper plate because he'll eat that, too, and I have another one who eats luncheon. And. That's. It.

Don't say 'They're not going to starve themselves' or 'Just force them to eat what's on their plate' or crap on about parents being the *reason* why kids are *like that*. I know you think you'll be different, but guess what — you won't be.

SIBLING RIVALRY

Watching my big boy dote on his baby brother was one of my favourite things to do. They just adored each other. My oldest wanted to help with everything. He kissed his baby brother on the forehead. Breathlessly told him he loved him all the time. He was gentle and caring. He raced into our bedroom every morning to see his brother. Every time the baby heard his big brother's voice his eyes lit up. His first smile was for his brother.

I am such a great parent, I thought. Really, these people whose kids fight like cats and dogs? They just need to be doing what I'm doing! I give attention to both children! I encourage them in building their bond! I nurture a great relationship between them! That's what you need to do.

I am a dick.

I was a dick.

I know better now. When the baby started crawling, things changed overnight. DON TOUCH MY FINGS! HE TOUCH MY FINGS! HE TOUCH MY TEDDY! STOP HIM! HE TOUCH MY KITCHEN! GET HIM AWAY! I DON WAN HIM IN MY ROOM! NO BABY! NO! GO AWAY! STOP DAT! MAAAAAAMA! STOP HIM. NOW! GO AWAY! HAERE ATU! (He even yells at him in te reo.)

This is my life now. Of course he liked his brother when he was a baby. *He didn't move.*

So that's just three times when I was smug when I shouldn't have been smug. Three out of a trillion times. Now I know, when I start thinking I have got something sussed I stop myself . . .

I know what's coming!

REMEMBER

We had a fight. A horrible one with lots of yelling.

Before we had children we outlined the type of parents we wanted to be. We found we fell on the same side for everything. Those silly little things we thought so important turned out not to be. They won't come into our bed, we said, before the reality of exhaustion set in, before we realised it's actually quite lovely to have your babies curled up next to you, safe and sound as the world carries on around you.

We said we wouldn't yell.

We made a No Yelling rule. And when we accidentally broke it our little enforcer would say 'HEY. WE IS A NO YELLING HOUSE!'

When watching the news once, Eddie saw John Key railing and said, 'His house is not a no yelling house isn't it?'

We had a fight and it was a horrible one.

With lots of yelling.

The tiredness — well, tiredness is too soft a word. The exhaustion. The bone-weariness. The way our bodies creak and our eyes hurt, and the dull thudding every morning . . . well, it got to us. It hit us like a sledgehammer.

I don't know what even started The Fight, but we couldn't be talked down from our respective cliffs as a gulf began to swell between us.

We started with a whisper and hiss but it became a roar.

And we were both so tired we couldn't back down.

Usually one would say — we are being silly. An arm outstretched saying *come to me, we are better than this*. A conciliatory sigh and then we would both apologise, a quick hug, a promise to talk later.

But not that day. Our world was too much and the walls were cracking and we were cracking and we yelled. We yelled out all of the frustration and fury and anger and the tiredness, the I AM SO FUCKING TIRED tiredness.

And neither of us could cross the gulf.

So we divided to organise the children. One to kindy and one for cuddles as a runny nose was taking over again — the main reason why we were falling apart at the seams.

When we returned to each other the rage was gone. Just sadness remained. That we'd not been able to talk ourselves down. To stop. I climbed into bed, my body aching. He took the baby for a drive.

Later we gingerly hugged each other, raw still from the words we didn't mean.

We went to pick up our son from kindy together and in the car we said to him: 'We're sorry we yelled this morning. We were very tired. But you shouldn't yell in anger at someone even when you're tired.'

'You was crying and yelling and it wasn't nice.'

'We were, and we're sorry, Eddie.'

'You need to remember you're best friends.'

And we looked at each other and smiled at our little boy who is wiser than us.

And we remembered.

Every day we choose each other. Every day we decide what kind of home we will make for our children and each other. In the chaos of parenting, when we are so tired every step feels like a marathon — we remember we're best friends. That we don't want to do this without each other. That not-sleeping every night with a baby between us is a life we choose to have together.

We remember that we're best friends.

And we will hold this — the next time our necks creak and we feel the anger rising, the next time the nausea of sleep deprivation swells, when there's another trigger, another action that seems thoughtless.

We will remember.

And we will choose a different path.

WHEN I GROW UP

We are the type of parents who should never be career advisors. Each day three-year-old Eddie approaches us with a new job that he wants to do. And we can't help but champion him.

'When I am a big. I am going have a job!'

'What will your job be, angel?'

'I'm gone be a gate!'

'Oh um, you'll be a wonderful gate! Umm, why do you want to be a gate?'

'So I can open and close!'

'Oh, of course . . .'

The next day . . .

'I am a new job!'

'Oh what is it?'

'I'm gone be a triangle when I growed up!'

'Play the triangle?'

'NO! BE a triangle. Don be silly you can't play a triangle dear Mama!'

'You'll be the best triangle there ever was, sweetheart!'

A few hours later:

'I'm going to be a mailbox so when people see me they get so happy because I'm full of birfday cards!'

Or:

'I'm going to be a ice-cream keeper but for babies when they come from when they're born!'

'Oh, a midwife/ice-cream maker/delivery person? Of course. That is definitely a thing you could be. If you deliver sushi to the post-natal ward you'd be really popular.'

THE WORLD IS BIG

My three-year-old talks about the world he will live in when he's 'big'. Big people drive cars. Big people don't go to school. Big people have jobs like being a garbage collepter or blowing up balloons or digging big holes or filling cups with water. Big people can go to the park whenever they like. Big people don't have to eat their dinner. Big people go out when it's dark. Big people go to bed whenever they want. There is a utopia in his mind of what life will be like when he is an adult. He cannot wait to be out in that big world when he's big. But I can wait.

I am scared. I see the news and I'm scared.

I'm scared of how big the world is.

I don't know how to parent in a world that is so big. A world that is so scary.

I struggle with the small stuff — how do I get him to eat his dinner? How do I get him to stop running off?

There's the stuff you think is bigger but it's not — how do you teach patience? Resilience?

The big stuff, the biggest stuff, is this: how do you protect them and protect others?

I know more kindness, more love, less entitlement, less hate is what we're told. And those words ring hollow sometimes. I try to take comfort from them, but it's so hard. How do we rise above slogans?

What can we as mothers do when the world is hurting? What can we as mothers of boys do about the fact that so much of the violence in this world is perpetrated by men in a culture of toxic and fragile masculinity?

This is not a post where there is an answer. It's not a post that ends with a cathartic laugh.

There's no joyous 'me too!'.

There's no snark here.

It's a call. Of some kind.

To make a world where all of our children are safe and all of our children keep others safe. I'm sure that's what we need for this big, big world.

We need a big heart for this big world.

I want to pledge now that I will parent knowing my child is going into this big world and he will have choices — choices to harm and hurt or to walk gently and powerfully with hope in his heart and love for others. I will parent knowing he is going into a world with your children, too, and that they need love and protection and respect. They need to be kept safe as I hope my son will be kept safe, too.

I pledge to always hold your children in my heart, too. To teach my children about consent, respect and unity. To teach them about their privilege and how that fits with their place in the world. I pledge to parent them with peace and in kindness in the hope that as they grow they treat others with peace and kindness.

I know I won't always get the small stuff right. But I'll try so hard to get the big stuff right. And in the face of so much brokenness, so much breathtaking sadness — what else can we do? What else can we do except say *Not here. Not my home. Not my children.*

I will pledge to love not only my children but all children. I will pledge to make my home a home for all. I will pledge to do something that brings words to life and into action.

Keep our children safe and keep the world safe.

What else can we do when the world is so big?

KID FIGHTS

eeee

I don't think there's anything more mind-numbingly infuriating than watching your toddler and preschooler fight. I mean, nothing does my head in more than seeing their inane arguments that are so completely unnecessary.

I've tried to see them from the point of view of the children. I've tried to remember I am a respectful parent who is reasonable and can understand that children don't see the world like adults do. But most of the time I'm just like — seriously, kids, can you not? Can you actually just not have this stupid fight?

It's always the same:

Toddler happily plays with thing.

Toddler makes eye contact with preschooler who is happily playing with other thing.

Toddler points at thing as if to say 'Do you want to come over and touch this thing that I'm happily playing with so that I can scream?'

Preschooler considers getting up to touch thing toddler is happily playing with. Instead they keep playing with the thing they're happily playing with.

Toddler grunts to get attention of preschooler. The grunt could easily be interpreted as 'Come over here and touch this thing I'm playing with, but also don't because if you do I will scream for 10 minutes.'

Preschooler puts down thing they're happily playing with, walks over and *takes* thing that toddler is happily playing with.

Toddler screams with righteous fury. Enough pitch at the highest level to sink a bloody ship.

Preschooler says 'What?'

How many times do we have to go through this? Just stop touching the bloody thing! Everybody needs to have their own thing and just play with that and leave everybody else's thing alone.

And when I say that, the kids just look at me like I'm mad.

Maybe I am.

Just play with your own thing, OK!

Everyone told me, when I only had one, that I'd need another. As if children were collectables. I was told that a second would mean my first would always have a friend.

It was true that in the beginning he was quite enamoured with his brother. Until the baby cried. Then I realised that having two very close together means the oldest is always waking up the youngest.

On day four of having two, my oldest baby decided his newborn brother was thirsty. So he poured his cup of juice all over him — while he was sleeping.

Other fun games have been:

How many books can I stack on the baby before he gets angry and flings the books back at me?

How many times in one day can I wake the baby?

How can I ensure Mama never has a warm coffee, ever? Not hot — just warm.

For a little while they were Best Friends Forever. Until the baby started moving. Then it was MINE MINE MINE MINE MINE.

And now that the baby is bigger still — it's HE PUSHED ME. And then the baby looking at me with a smug grin like DID NOT.

And you know he did.

I sit them at opposite ends of the room to eat. They're constantly spear-tackling each other. And toys are always flying through the air.

The other day the room was absolute chaos — screaming

and projectiles and screeching laughter and domination through force on both sides (they're more evenly matched now — one is tall and skinny, one is short and chubby) — and as I was about to pull my hair out my husband walked in the door.

He surveyed the scene and began to smile. I guess he likes his lounge being turned into a gladiator's arena.

He jumped in with them and began to wrestle.

I took the opportunity to sit in the bathroom with a packet of chips and my phone. I began Googling pictures of Alexander Skarsgard. I could hear them screeching with delight upstairs.

There's no way I'm having a third, I thought.

Then as I heard my husband's booming laugh . . . I thought . . . well . . . maybe.

'MIIIIIIINE!'

Definitely.

SLEEPOVER

~⌣

We told Eddie if he kept managing to get up during the night for the toilet he could have a sleepover — the one request he's had for months.

'You can have your very best friend for a sleepover. You can only have one friend though, so think very carefully and tell us when you're ready.'

'I already know who I want!'

'Oh, OK — who?'

'My baby brova. He's my very best friend.'

GOING BACK TO WORK

Oh, the life of a working mum. I don't even know where to begin.

I remember being equal parts fear and excitement at returning to work.

I didn't want to leave my son, but I did.

I knew I'd miss him, but I was also looking forward to pooping alone.

I craved adult conversation, but I was scared I wouldn't be able to actually *have* an adult conversation.

I wanted to dress in nice clothes and be well presented after months in maternity leggings, but the idea of wearing proper clothes just exhausted me.

I was excited about not breastfeeding all day, but so not looking forward to pumping.

I was worried my boobs would leak through my clothes during a meeting (they did).

I was worried I'd fall asleep during the day. (I once did go into a meeting room to catch up on paperwork before my next meeting and promptly fell asleep for 10 minutes. I woke with a drool trail that went to my shoulder.)

I was worried my son wouldn't cope without me (he did).

I was worried my husband wouldn't like being a stay-at-home dad (he liked it as much as I did, as in he liked it but not all the time — as is the case with all stay-at-home parents).

Most of all I was worried I'd miss my child's life.

And I missed bits of it, it's true. But I was doing what I needed to be doing. Which was to provide for my family. My husband had missed moments in the first part of our son's life while he had worked. We all miss bits.

But the bits I missed meant we could pay the bills. Meant we could pay the rent and my son could have swimming lessons and thermal clothes for winter, and it meant my husband could be an at-home parent, too, something neither of us felt he should miss out on just because his name is Dad and not Mum.

Going back to work the first time around was one of the hardest things I've ever done. I look back now and wonder how I coped.

I'd love to be able to provide you with a list of how to do it. All the tips! All the ways to get more out of your day.

Sorry . . .

I made mistakes. Like working too many hours. Like pushing myself too hard because I wanted a pay rise. Like not appreciating my husband who was at home doing *heaps* of work.

I made heaps of mistakes and you will, too.

And that's OK.

If I could change anything or advise you on any one thing to do when returning to work it would be this:

Be kind to yourself.

It's hard. And you are doing your best and some days your best won't be enough, but most of the time it will be.

You can do it all but you don't have to. Having it all sometimes means having the things that are most important to you and leaving the rest.

You'll fuck up. We all do. Whether we are at home or at work. But your baby will still run to the door when you get home. They'll still race to you when you pick them up from day care.

It'll feel like Groundhog Day and you'll be exhausted, but you'll do it. And you'll do it really fucking well some days.

Don't rush yourself, because it will take time to get a rhythm, and some days the band will start playing a different song and you won't have the energy to dance to it.

Remember you're achieving. It might not look perfect and it doesn't have to be. You might feel judged because people are dickheads.

But the bigger picture is this: you're making something for you and for your family. This is how you are being the best mum you can be. Everyone's picture looks different. You're doing your best and that's enough. It's more than enough.

Now get to that meeting, I believe in you (but wipe the baby puke off your shoulder).

YOU'VE GOT THIS

I know it doesn't feel like it today, but you do.

I know the baby didn't sleep all night. They kept waking and your back was aching from rocking and shushing and rocking and shushing.

And I know you said things under your breath or in your head and when they finally fell asleep, tiny bubbles of sweat on their little noses, skin clammy and cheeks hot — I know you thought to yourself that you shouldn't have said those things.

You need to know that it's OK. It's OK that you hissed in the darkness or you let out an angry plea or you swore. It's OK.

You've got this.

I know it doesn't feel like it, and you're exhausted, and you feel like you need to do better.

But I know you've got this.

Your baby slept. And they slept safe and warm in their beds and it might have only been for a few hours or maybe four if you're lucky or maybe it was only 45 minutes.

But they slept in peace, surrounded by your love, in the home you made for them.

You've got this, mama.

When they woke and you were so tired but you still got up to them and you went into their room and you smiled wide as their eyes searched for you, as their arms reached for you.

You lifted them into a soft and gentle embrace and you whispered 'I love you' even though your feet were dragging and your shoulders felt like the weight of the world was on them and your eyes could barely open.

You've got this, mama.

Because their body calmed in your arms, and they stopped crying because nobody loves them like you do and they know this.

And they'll cry again, and you won't know why. And you'll say the list of — dry and clean and hungry? No — must be tired. Or is it teeth? And it won't matter, because tomorrow it will be something different.

And you'll snap sometimes and you'll leave them crying in their cot while you take some deep breaths. Or you'll take one more sip of cold coffee. You'll blink back tears. And that's OK.

That's what being a mum is.

And your baby won't see this now and when they're grown they won't remember the times when you said Just. Please. Stop. Crying. With a sharp edge to your voice. Or when you yelled JUST GO THE FUCK TO SLEEP! And you felt so guilty. So guilty.

They won't remember.

And neither will you.

They'll just remember that they were warm and safe and you loved them, oh how you loved them.

You loved them so much that you kept loving them even more every single day.

That's what they'll remember.

You've got this, mama.